ENCYCLOPEDIA
NEUROTICA

ALSO BY JON WINOKUR

The War Between the State
The Traveling Curmudgeon
How to Win at Golf Without Actually Playing Well
Advice to Writers
Happy Motoring (with Norrie Epstein)
The Rich Are Different
Je Ne Sais What?
Fathers
The Portable Curmudgeon Redux
True Confessions
Mondo Canine
Friendly Advice
A Curmudgeon's Garden of Love
Zen to Go
The Portable Curmudgeon
Writers on Writing

ENCYCLOPEDIA
NEUROTICA

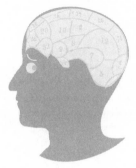

Jon Winokur

ST. MARTIN'S PRESS
NEW YORK

www.stmartins.com

Book design by Jonathan Bennett

Library of Congress Cataloging-in-Publication Data

Winokur, Jon.
    Encyclopedia neurotica / Jon Winokur.—1st ed.
        p. cm.
    Includes index (p. 263).
    ISBN 0-312-32500-2
    EAN 978-0312-32500-8
    1. Neurotics—Humor. 2. Neuroses—Humor. 3. American wit and humor. I. Title.

    PN6231.N55W56 2005
    818'.607—dc22

                                                        2004051245

First Edition: January 2005

10   9   8   7   6   5   4   3   2   1

For my parents. No kidding.

Everybody's a screwball in some way.
That doesn't make them crazy.
—STANLEY ROBERTS

FOREWORD

Inasmuch as I haven't slept in weeks after Jon Winokur guilt-tripped me into writing this foreword for his new, extraordinarily authentic work, I feel better knowing that he probably chose the right person.

Since I can begin my fearful attempt in any number of a million ways, certainly a phobia that is in this tome somewhere (or should be; "Foreword Fear" perhaps?), I might as well just dive in as blindly as I was raised as a child.

I loved my childhood. Sadly, it hated me.

I take full responsibility now, after recently terminating over three decades of psychotherapy, for my parents' screwing me up for life. It's not their fault that they didn't have the "tools." I'm certain their own grandparents back in the late 1890s probably told their own parents things like, "You don't clean a musket like that, you schmuck!" And they were human—perhaps their biggest flaw. Of course, the Lewis heritage is not so different from most families, Jewish or otherwise—other than some of my relatives literally opening up "side shows" and charging admission for the public to be able to watch me and my cousins' adolescence go down the tubes. It's fair to say that many of the relatives (all of whom insisted on being referred to as "distant") had deeply rooted emotional problems that hindered their own self-esteem and made them poster men and women for Mr. Winokur's "encyclopedia from hell." To cite just a few examples: one of my aunts *knitted her own suicide note*, an uncle, in his will, *left his grief to science*, my mother, a legendary hypochondriac, *used to eat M&Ms, one at a time, with water*, and my grandfather had such bad breath we had to leave *after-death mints* by his graveside yearly after a poltergeist advocacy group complained to the cemetery board of directors. Suffice it to say I came from problems, I have problems, and my biggest concern is that after I die my problems don't get anywhere near the hearse.

This book is for Everyman and Everywoman to give to every kid out of a sense of duty. Forget how entertaining it is—had I, as a child, had the opportunity to read a book like *Encyclopedia Neurotica*, I would have had a running start on what turned out to be a fabulously tormented existence.

With any luck, when this volume hits the stands, I will be close to nearly a decade of sobriety. Although I tried to chronicle my demons in my memoir, *The Other Great Depression*, it has only been of late that I've realized that by turning my life around so positively, I have gotten so much clarity that I despise myself even more. And yet, I am a grateful—and sober—basket case.

I read this book again and again with glee, feeling so much more a part of society and not as fearful of having the vast majority of these entries all to myself. My maturity was evident, unlike in the past when I was given a book on eating disorders and I promptly ate the book. This time I read it like a mature, middle-aged man and then helped other addicts, did some charity, worked on my stand-up, and ended the day by masturbating my usual three hundred times. Doesn't get much better than that.

Enjoy the read. If you don't spot yourself in at least half this book, be quite certain that you are not human.

—Richard Lewis
Hollywood, California

ACKNOWLEDGMENTS

I wish to thank Elizabeth Beier, Peter Bell, Bruce Bellingham, Tony Bill, Reid Boates, Norman Corwin, Marshall Danien, Norrie Epstein, Larry Gelbart, Bryan Gordon, Dewey Gram, Florence King, Lucy Lee, Richard Lewis, Howard Ogden, Al Rasof, Jane Rosenman, Sam Williams, and Elinor Winokur for their various contributions. Though of course *I* did all the work. But people expect to be thanked, so you have to keep track of everyone who sent you a clipping or recommended a book or lent you money or talked you out of killing yourself, and you're terrified you'll leave somebody out because you don't want to *offend.* Why can't people just let you work? No, they have to see their names in print.

Happy now?

Note to the reader: Some of the quotations in this book do not carry sources and/or dates because, over several decades of collecting quotations, I was not always diligent in recording that vital information. My editors urged me to track it all down, but I decided that to do so would be an unhealthy exercise in compulsivity. Be assured, however, that all attributions are accurate.

—JW

INTRODUCTION

This book is an irreverent guide to the wacky world of neurosis, that safety-valve craziness that shields us from the Abyss, those sundry tics and twitches that stave off insanity. It proceeds from the conviction that Western culture has gone terribly wrong in its view of the human condition, that the pervading "therapeutic ethos" wrongly pathologizes deviant behavior with pseudoscientific "diagnoses" and mistakenly labels eccentricities as "disorders." It suggests that rather than medicalizing our oddness, we should accept, appreciate, and even delight in it, because lunacy has definite entertainment value, at least when it doesn't hurt anyone (and occasionally when it does). "The nice thing about Southerners is the way we enjoy our neuroses," writes Florence King, and I think we could all profit from their example.

Postmodern life was overwhelming enough before September 11, 2001, when the world plunged into a new Age of Anxiety. Now our psyches are fraught with even more angst, ambivalence, and dread. From this well of worry flows a torrent of bizarre behavior. The old standbys are still thriving—depression, addiction, unresolved anger—and new complexes, phobias, and compulsions are surfacing all the time. To add to this reservoir of *mishegoss,* in the twenty-first century, bad habits have been turned into diseases, foibles are afflictions, and sins are syndromes.

We're concerned here with neurosis in the colloquial sense, not limited by arbitrary clinical definitions, nor by New Age drivel, nor Freudian filth. We unblinkingly examine the fascinating vagaries of human behavior, including the creepy, the kinky, even the mildly criminal. We avoid psychosis, however, because there's nothing cute about being hospitalized and medicated because you can't stop the voices in your head. No, our subjects here are the walking wounded, people who have serious "issues" but still manage to function, more or less. In other words, the vast majority of the human race.

We're all a bit twisted, are we not? And isn't that a *good* thing, really? Maybe a little nuttiness displaces a lot of insanity. Isn't it better to be slightly peculiar than completely deranged? Or, almost as bad, boringly sane? Sanity, if it exists, is dull and predictable. The aberrations make life interesting. They give us character (and characters, from Oedipus to the Odd Couple, Hamlet to Harry Potter). No matter how bizarre or inconvenient, they make us more elaborate, more fascinating, more charming, more . . . human. Or, as Carrie Fisher says, "All the good people are nuts."

Join us, then, as we sail the seas of anxiety, shoot the rapids of rage, scuba the depths of depression, gaze into the reflecting pools of narcissism, fishtail on the oily puddles of addiction, cruise the confluence of addiction and codependency. . . .

Sorry, sometimes I get carried away.

—Jon Winokur
Pacific Palisades, California

A

Note: words in *italics* within definitions will also be found as separate entries.

Absurd, the

Literally "out of harmony," the bewildering state of existence in a purposeless universe.

> Why does a person even get up in the morning? You have breakfast, you floss your teeth so you'll have healthy gums in your old age, and then you get in your car and drive down I-10 and die. Life is so stupid I can't stand it.
>
> —Barbara Kingsolver

> The absurd is born of the confrontation between the human call and the unreasonable silence of the world.
>
> —Albert Camus, *The Myth of Sisyphus* (1942)

> I hope life isn't a big joke, because I don't get it.
>
> —Jack Handey

See also *catch-22, human condition, Myth of Sisyphus.*

"abuse" abuse

Indiscriminate use of the word "abuse" as the second element of a compound, referring either to the thing misused, or the thing or person harmed, as in "fragrance abuse" (wearing too much perfume), "laxative abuse" (excessive purging as part of an *eating disorder*), "racket abuse" (see *McEnroe, John*), "river abuse" (riparian pollution), and "math abuse" (figures lie and liars figure).

Abyss, the
Literally, the bottomless pit of primeval chaos from which the universe was formed; figuratively, the yawning, unfathomable chasm of existential terror.

> Whoever fights monsters should see to it that in the process he does not become a monster. And when you look long into an abyss, the abyss also looks into you.
>
> —Friedrich Nietzsche

See also *angst, dark night of the soul, undertoad.*

acquired situational narcissism
An adult-onset form of *narcissism* characterized by grandiosity, lack of empathy, *rage,* isolation, and substance abuse. According to Cornell Medical School psychiatrist Robert Millman, acquired situational narcissism mainly afflicts celebrities, who tend to be surrounded by *enablers.*

addiction (formerly "habit")
Compulsive need for a habit-forming substance such as nicotine, alcohol, or heroin. Some psychologists hold that applying the word *addiction* to compulsive behaviors involving sex, overeating, or gambling dilutes the meaning of a term that should be reserved for biogenetic diseases like alcoholism.
See also *plastic surgery addiction.*

> Addiction has become one of the cant terms to explain less-desired behavior of all sorts. In the 1950s, when I was growing up, addiction meant horrible obsession and dealt almost exclu-

sively with drugs, usually alcohol. With the rise of the self-help
movement addiction has come to describe a less-pleasing behavior than one might like. You can now be addicted to chocolate,
video games, procrastination, late night TV, sex, eating and/or
not eating, and buying expensive things you don't need.
—James B. Twitchell, *Living It Up:*
Our Love Affair with Luxury (2002)

Could it be that by labeling common problems addictions we're
actually magnifying their power over us and making it even
harder to conquer them?
—*Utne Reader,* November–December 1988

addiction memoir
Increasingly popular literary genre (or at least book category) in
which the authors congratulate themselves for their triumphs
over substance abuse.
See also *celebrity sufferer.*

adolescent
One who suffers from hormone-induced dementia.

Weird clothing is de rigueur for teenagers, but today's generation
of teens is finding it difficult to be sufficiently weird . . . because
the previous generation, who went through adolescence in the six-
ties and seventies, used up practically all the available weirdness.
—P. J. O'Rourke, *Modern Manners* (1990)

adultolescent
Person between the ages of twenty-five and thirty-four who lives
with his parents. The 2000 U.S. Census counted four million adultolescents, and according to another survey, 60 percent of college
students plan to live at home after graduation. Independence is

thus no longer a universal goal, and "living at home" after college is no longer stigmatized.

> The conveyor belt that once transported adolescents into adulthood has broken down.
>
> —Frank Furstenberg, sociologist

See also *scaffolding*.

adult temper tantrum

No longer the exclusive domain of small children, the temper tantrum is now acceptable grownup behavior, and not just for athletes and celebrities: Some management experts actually offer tips on how to lose your temper at the office for maximum advantage. Owen Edwards, author of *Upward Nobility: How to Succeed in Business Without Losing Your Soul,* claims that "a good old-fashioned temper tantrum can send the message to others that you aren't willing to be pushed around," and suggests that some bosses have a grudging respect for employees who know how to throw well-timed tantrums. But mental health professionals say that temper tantrums do nothing but alienate and frighten those around you, and can be hazardous to your health. The adult temper tantrum has been elevated to cinematic art by Jack Nicholson.

5 FILMS WITH CLASSIC JACK NICHOLSON TEMPER TANTRUMS
per Michael Wilmington, Chicago Tribune *movie critic*

---

1. The Chicken Salad Tantrum in *Five Easy Pieces*
(Bob Rafelson; 1970)
In a diner, Bobby Dupea (Nicholson) orders toast with his eggs. When a rude waitress says it's unavailable, he orders chicken

(continued)

salad on toast, then asks her to "Hold the chicken." "You want me to hold the chicken?" she growls. "I want you to hold it between your knees!" Bobby explodes, before sweeping the table clean.

2. The Housekeeping Fit in *Carnal Knowledge*
(Mike Nichols; 1971)
Jack's best: Before a party, cynical New Yorker Jonathan (Nicholson) confronts girlfriend Bobbie's (Ann-Margret) teary complaints that she sleeps all day because she has nothing to do. "You want a job? Fix up this pigsty! Try vacuuming!" He then hits a red-faced crescendo. "That's why you can hardly stand up! This place smells like a coffin!"

3. The Barroom Blowup in *The Last Detail*
(Hal Ashby; 1973)
A surly bartender refuses to serve Meadows (Randy Quaid), the navy convict Billy Buddusky (Nicholson) is escorting to Portsmouth—and then threatens to call the Shore Patrol. Buddusky unleashes a torrent of profanity. "Shore Patrol? You're gonna call the Shore Patrol? Listen . . . I *am* the Shore Patrol! Now, give this guy a beer!"

4. The Barbershop Tiff in *Chinatown*
(Roman Polanski; 1974)
Seeking a peaceful haircut and shave, L.A. private eye J. J. Gittes (Nicholson) is riled by a fellow customer's nasty critique of his most recent case. Rising from his chair, Gittes tongue-lashes the other customer ("I don't kick them out of their homes like you jerks who work in the bank!") until the barber distracts him with a joke.

(continued)

5. The Last Crackup in *The Shining*
(Stanley Kubrick; 1980)
At a snowbound lodge, wife Wendy (Shelley Duvall) discovers
her alcoholic writer–blocked spouse Jack (Nicholson) has gone
mad. Trying to save herself and son from the longest tantrum in
any Nicholson movie, she locks herself in a closet, which he de-
stroys with ax blows, capped with his blood-chilling peekaboo.
"Heeere's Johnny!"

affluenza
Virus of affluence that psychotherapist Jessie H. O'Neill defines
as "the collective addictions, character flaws, psychological wounds,
neuroses, and behavioral disorders caused or exacerbated by the
presence of, or desire for, wealth." Affluenza victims, regardless
of their socioeconomic level, falsely believe that money can solve
all their problems. Other symptoms include feelings of hopelessness, low *self-esteem,* inability to delay gratification, low frustration tolerance, workaholism, and feelings of isolation and
separation. According to O'Neill, affluenza is not only highly
contagious, it is also hereditary.

> Americans become unhappy and vicious because their preoccu-
> pation with amassing possessions obliterates their loneliness.
> This is why production in America seems to be on such an
> endless upward spiral: every time we buy something we deepen
> our emotional deprivation and hence our need to buy some-
> thing.
>
> —Philip Slater, *Wealth Addiction* (1980)

In our view, the affluenza epidemic is rooted in the fact that our supreme measure of national progress is that quarterly ring of the cash register we call the Gross Domestic Product. It's rooted in the idea that every generation will be materially more wealthy than its predecessor, and that, somehow, each of us can pursue that single-minded end without damaging the countless other things we hold dear.

> —John de Graaf, David Wann, and Thomas H. Naylor,
> *Affluenza: The All-Consuming Epidemic* (2001)

See also *hedonistic treadmill.*

Age of Anxiety, the

Appellation bestowed on the twentieth century by the poet W. H. Auden in his book-length poem of the same title which won a Pulitzer Prize in 1948.

> Our Age of Anxiety is, in great part, the result of trying to do today's jobs with yesterday's tools.
>
> —Marshall McLuhan

agita

Dyspepsia, Italian-style.

agoraphobia

Greek for "fear of the marketplace." The agoraphobe fears crowds, lines, trains, planes, cars—any situation that might trigger a *panic attack.*

> The recluse imagines that if he can reduce the possibility of surprises the world will become orderly, but the more order he contrives, the more it is vulnerable to fortune. The wish to elim-

inate chance leads to the madness of which method is the symptom.

—Frederic Raphael, *Eyes Wide Open: A Memoir of Stanley Kubrick* (1999)

See also *loner, recluse, solitude.*

alcoholic (formerly "drunkard," "alky" "lush," "rummy," "dipsomaniac," "wino," "sot," "booze-hound," "barfly")
Someone who drinks to excess as a result of the disease of alcoholism. It was once thought that problem-drinking was a failure of willpower, but since the advent of 12-Step programs, the idea that alcoholics are powerless over their addiction has become an article of faith.

If the headache would only precede the intoxication, alcoholism would be a virtue.

—Samuel Butler

When I was a practicing alcoholic, I was unbelievable. One side effect was immense suspicion: I'd come off tour like Inspector Clouseau on acid. Where'd this cornflake come from? It wasn't here before.

—Ozzy Osbourne

I have taken more out of alcohol than alcohol has taken out of me.

—Winston Churchill

alexithymia
Alleged *disorder* that prevents its victims from expressing their *feelings.* As if that were a problem.

Allen, Woody (Allen Stuart Konigsberg, 1935-)

Short, insecure, self-absorbed, ambivalent, Jewish, and funny, Woody Allen was America's favorite neurotic until he dumped Mia Farrow for her twenty-one-year-old adopted daughter.

He contributed gags to a newspaper column while still in high school and became a comedy writer for Sid Caesar after graduation. At twenty-three he began performing his own material and was soon a popular stand-up. He wrote humorous essays for the *New Yorker* that he published in three anthologies, and wrote his first screenplay, *What's New Pussycat?*, in 1965, but so abhorred the Hollywood experience that he resolved never to work in that town again. The movie, however, made money and Allen was suddenly bankable, and he went on to direct a long string of "personal films" about his twin torments, sex and death, and became a rarity in the American cinema: an independent auteur. He appeared in most of his films as a wisecracking New Yorker, a nerdy, quasi-intellectual *kvetch*. In the process he became the world's most famous analysand who perhaps did more for *Freud* than a whole convention of psychoanalysts.

After two failed marriages, Allen's relationship with Diane Keaton inspired his first serious film, *Annie Hall*, which won the Best Picture Oscar in 1977. The disastrous split with Farrow occurred after she discovered "pornographic Polaroids" of her twenty-one-year-old adopted daughter Soon-Yi Previn in his apartment (he was fifty-seven at the time). Asked about the propriety of the relationship, his only explanation was, "The heart wants what it wants." He has since tried to rehabilitate his public image by making himself more accessible to the press and by allowing a documentary film crew to follow him on a tour of Europe with his Dixieland band, but for those who loved his early work, the Wood Man, alas, just isn't funny anymore.

With me, it's a genetic dissatisfaction with everything.
—Woody Allen

Daily life for this brilliant, courteous man seems to be a matter
of endlessly fending off guilt, which settles on the balconies of
his intellect like the pigeons on the terraces of his apartment.

—Penelope Gilliatt, *The New Yorker*

He has been called the modern version of Chaplin's Little
Man, yanked into the Age of Anxiety. But that's only part of
it. More than any contemporary performer, Allen has turned
nervousness and insecurity into an art form. Beset by fears of
death—remember him shopping for books on death while Annie Hall looks for books on cats?—he's not much more secure
when it comes to sex, or the ability to believe that any pleasure
can be more than fleeting, and in any case thoroughly undeserved.

—Jay Carr, *The Boston Globe,* March 5, 1989

Woody Allen didn't even buy sheets without talking to his psychiatrist. I know that several sessions went into his switch from
polyester-satin to cotton.

—Mia Farrow, *What Falls Away* (1997)

If I were building a statue to Dr. Freud, and I were going to put
it in New York, and the statue was going to be Freud in his office, it would be Woody Allen on the couch.

—Edward Koch, former mayor of New York

ambient fear
Background *anxiety* of everyday life.
See also *free-floating anxiety.*

ambiguity
Dubiousness; uncertainty; vagueness.

Neurosis is the inability to tolerate ambiguity.

—Sigmund Freud

See also *ambivalence, doubt.*

ambivalence (formerly "confusion")

Coexistence of contradictory ideas, attitudes, or feelings, such as love and hate, toward a person, an object, or a situation, which may or may not be fully conscious.

I arise in the morning torn between a desire to improve the world and a desire to enjoy the world. This makes it hard to plan the day.

—E. B. White

Part of me suspects that I'm a loser, and the other part of me thinks I'm God Almighty.

—John Lennon

The test of a first-rate intelligence is the ability to hold two opposed ideas in the mind at the same time, and still retain the ability to function.

—F. Scott Fitzgerald, *The Crack-Up* (1945)

anal retentive personality (formerly "tidy")

One who is excessively meticulous and orderly. According to psychoanalytic theory, the anal retentive personality results from guilt and anxiety caused by early efforts to control bowel movements, which the child finds pleasurable. Go figure.

I'm full of fears and I do my best to avoid difficulties and any kind of complications. I like everything around me to be clear as crystal and completely calm. I don't want clouds overhead. I get a feeling of inner peace from a well-organized desk. When I take a bath, I put everything neatly back in place. You wouldn't even know I'd been in the bathroom. My passion for orderliness goes hand in hand with a strong revulsion toward complications.

—Alfred Hitchcock

People try to tell you that the secret to pepper steak is the season-ing—but we know different, don't we? Uh-huh. It's getting all the pieces the same size. And that's what I've done here. Beaut—Uh-oh. This one's a little bigger than the rest, so we'll just discard that one . . . and I don't think this little wrinkly one belongs in here . . . and this, well, I just don't like the look of that one at all. In fact, why don't we just start over and throw this out.

—Phil Hartman
as "The Anal Retentive Chef" on *Saturday Night Live*

The apartment was plastered with photos of naked men. One showed a penis as long as my arm. There was a whip stand in the bedroom and hardware on the walls and a stack of *Meatmen* magazines on the back of the toilet. Yet, the house was unbe-lievably orderly. These guys were so anal they alphabetized their laundry products: All, Bold, Cheer, Dash, Fab.

—Louise Rafkin, *Other People's Dirt* (1998)

ANAL RETENTIVE HALL OF FAME

William Randolph Hearst accumulated a substantial percentage of the world's art to decorate his California castle but kept most of it in warehouses.

Mark McCormack, founder and chairman of a worldwide sports management company, monitored his goals and accomplishments

(continued)

on a series of index cards and kept careful track of sleep, exercise, and time spent with his family.

The Viennese novelist Arthur Schnitzler, whose *Traumnovelle (Dream Story*, 1926) was the basis for Stanley Kubrick's last film, *Eyes Wide Shut* (1999), kept precise count of every orgasm he ever had.

Head of the Nazi SS Heinrich Himmler, who oversaw the slaughter of millions, diligently recorded all his haircuts, shaves, and baths.

National Football League wide receiver Jerry Rice tries to exert absolute control over his environment. He's a meticulous dresser on and off the field whose pregame routine takes two hours. "Before the game, I'll take a towel, wipe my helmet off to get it all shiny to go out there and get banged around," he says. He maintains a spotless house, perfectly organized closets, and a surgically clean car. "I can't breathe if it's not neat. I don't feel comfortable," he says.

Martha Stewart reportedly dusts the tops of her doors, reads her cookbooks front to back, and always tears her English muffins (because her equally meticulous father taught her never to slice them).

Martha Stewart's house is not the biggest one on her street in Westport, Connecticut, but the shrubbery gives away its owner. The bushes aren't just wrapped in burlap, the ne plus ultra of winterization; the fabric has been tailored to fit the precise dimensions of each plant. . . . Her kitchen is dense with Stewart-touches: forty-eight gleaming copper pots hang above the stove, hundreds of antique dishes fill the glass-fronted cabinets, and the dish-washing liquid is decanted into a glass cruet beside the sink.

—Jeffrey Toobin, "Lunch at Martha's,"
The New Yorker, February 3, 2003

"Tidy" is a dear little word, and Miss Manners is sorry to find it pass out of use. Swept under the rug, as it were.

It is true that we have other ways of referring to people who enjoy keeping things neat, who pick up after themselves without being threatened, and who maintain their homes nicely for themselves and other residents, instead of making desperate swipes at order only when guests are expected.

But the modern terms for "tidy" don't have the same charm. Miss Manners doesn't care for either "compulsive" or "control freak."

Even less does she care for the modern habit of redefining good habits as signs of bad character. It is clever to declare one's weakness a virtue and demand to be not just forgiven for one's lapses, but admired. However, this ploy is done at the expense of the dutiful, who are made to feel sheepish and apologetic about doing the right thing. . . .

The notion that messiness is a warm and endearing trait, while orderliness is freakish enjoys amazing success. Even people who truly love order commonly refer disparagingly to their own good habits.

—Miss Manners (Judith Martin),
Chicago Tribune, March 26, 1998

anglolalia
The uncontrollable urge to affect a British accent, most often afflicting celebrities (Madonna, Faye Dunaway, Sammy Davis Jr.,

Kathleen Turner, Jessye Norman) and, for some reason, Reform rabbis.

angst
German for a kind of fearful worry, a deep, existential *anxiety*.

> Man is the only animal for whom his own existence is a problem that he has to solve.
> —Erich Fromm, *Man for Himself* (1947)

> More than any other time in history, mankind faces a crossroads. One path leads to despair and utter hopelessness. The other, to total extinction. Let us pray we have the wisdom to choose correctly.
> —Woody Allen, *Side Effects* (1980)

See also *abyss, dark night of the soul, human condition, undertoad.*

Annie Hall
Billed as "a nervous romance," the winner of the 1977 Oscar for Best Picture is named for its neurotic protagonist, who is based on the neurotic actress who plays her (see *Keaton, Diane*), brought to the screen by a neurotic director (see *Allen, Woody*).

antidepressant
Class of drugs (including Prozac, Paxil, Zoloft, and Effexor) that alter the brain's chemistry by increasing serotonin levels. The use of antidepressants has skyrocketed, with 6.3 million Americans taking them in 2002, yielding huge profits for the pharmaceutical industry. Critics say they're prescribed too readily and that potential side effects are not sufficiently known.

> The antidepressants are basically speed.
> —Ronald Leifer, M.D.

Were Moses to go up Mt. Sinai today, the two tablets he'd bring down with him would be aspirin and Prozac.
                                        —Joseph A. Califano Jr.

See also *Prozac.*

antique diagnosis
Psychopathologies such as "the vapours," hysteria, *neurasthenia, railway neurosis,* catatonia, or nervous prostration, which are no longer believed to exist. Indeed, the description and classification of mental disorders is an ever-shifting landscape, and most psychological theories are eventually refuted.

anxiety
Worry, uneasiness, tension, apprehension. More Americans see doctors for anxiety than for colds. Experts say there is no evidence that anxiety is any more common than before, but is simply no longer ignored by health professionals. In fact, the problem has been known for decades: The Victorians called it "the vapours," in the 1950s it was known as "atypical depression," and in the 1970s "endogenous anxiety."

Some amount of never-ending anxiety may be rational, keeping us on guard. Perhaps anxiety is even hardwired into us by evolution, as the most fretful of our ancestors (the ones always warily scanning the horizon) were the ones who survived and passed their attitudes down to us.
                                        —Gregg Easterbrook, *The Progress Paradox:*
                                        How Life Gets Better While People Feel Worse (2003)

In headaches and in worry
Vaguely life leaks away.
                                        —W. H. Auden, "Another Time" (1940)

How strange it is. We have these deep terrible lingering fears about ourselves and the people we love. Yet we walk around, talk to people, eat, and drink. We manage to function. The feelings are deep and real. Shouldn't they paralyze us? How is it we can survive them, at least for a while? We drive a car, we teach a class. How is it no one sees how deeply afraid we were, last night, this morning? Is it something we all hide from each other, by mutual consent? Or do we share the same secret without knowing it? Wear the same disguise?

—Don DeLillo, *White Noise* (1985)

There is no such thing as pure pleasure; some anxiety always goes with it.

—Ovid, *Metamorphoses*

Nerves provide me with energy. They work for me. It's when I don't have them, when I feel at ease, that I get worried.

—Mike Nichols

People wish to be settled; only as far as they are unsettled is there any hope for them.

—Ralph Waldo Emerson, *Essays: First Series* (1841)

Stupidity is without anxiety.

—Johann Wolfgang von Goethe

Gentiles don't know how to worry.

—Stanley Kubrick

See also *generalized anxiety disorder, stage fright.*

apathy
Lack of feeling, emotion, or concern about important matters.

I DON'T KNOW. I DON'T CARE. AND IT DOESN'T
MAKE ANY DIFFERENCE.

—Jack Kerouac

apocalyptic babble
Drumbeat warnings from TV preachers that *the world is coming to an end! Soon! So send money!*

As Good As It Gets
A movie written and directed by James L. Brooks, starring Jack Nicholson as an *Obsessive Compulsive Disorder* sufferer who won't eat with restaurant silverware, refuses to step on sidewalk cracks, and must wear gloves to make physical contact with other people.

ataque de nervios
"Attack of the nerves," a syndrome recognized in Hispanic cultures and roughly equivalent to anxiety and depressive disorders. See also *nervous breakdown*.

Attention-Deficit/Hyperactivity Disorder (ADHD)
Range of supposed disorders exhibited by children, especially boys, characterized by "hyperactivity," inattentiveness, distractibility, impulsiveness, fidgeting, and squirming.

No one explains where this disease came from, why it didn't exist fifty years ago. No one is able to diagnose it with objective tests. It's diagnosed by a teacher complaining or a parent complaining. People are referring to the fact that they don't like misbehaving children, mainly boys, in the schools. The diagnosis helps tranquilize the parent, tranquilize the school system. It offers them the sense that they are doing something about the problem, that they are dealing with it in a rational, scientific way. It's a kind of pharmacological magic.

—Thomas Szasz, "Curing the Therapeutic State"

See also *Ritalin.*

autosuggestion
See *self-affirmation.*

B

bad choices
Psychobabble for "dumb mistakes."

bad seed
A congenitally evil child, from *The Bad Seed,* Maxwell Anderson's play about a murderous little girl based on William March's novel of the same title.

Barnum statement
Trick used by astrologers, fortune-tellers, psychics, and psychologists based on P. T. Barnum's dictum, "A circus should have a little something for everyone." Thus a carefully worded statement about an individual, if based on universal personality traits, is almost always accepted as an accurate assessment by the person so described, a phenomenon that renders most personality studies inherently inaccurate.

bashful bladder syndrome
Psychophysiological urinary problem also called paruresis in which the patient has difficulty urinating in public lavatories, or at the home of friends or relatives, or in his own home if some-

one is waiting to use the bathroom. Sufferers employ a variety of coping strategies, including running water to promote urination, limiting fluid intake, and avoiding public rest rooms altogether.

battle of the sexes, the
Endless strife caused by the inherent differences between men and women.

> Men get their identity from their work, women get their identity from their men.
> —Carrie Fisher, *The Portable Curmudgeon Redux* (1992)

> Men don't get enough sex and women don't get enough love.
> —Terry Lee Goodrich,
> *Fort Worth Star-Telegram*, December 11, 1991

> Yes, men don't get enough sex because women don't get enough love, but women don't get enough love because men don't get enough sex.
> —"Don," thirty-nine-year-old manufacturing manager,
> quoted by Terry Lee Goodrich,
> *Fort Worth Star-Telegram*, December 11, 1991

beer goggles
Effect of intoxication on one's standards for the opposite sex. In an attempt to quantify the phenomenon, a Glasgow University *study* found that after three beers, both men and women perceived members of the opposite sex as precisely 25 percent more attractive than before they started drinking.

bestiality
Sexual relations between a human and an animal. Though frowned upon by most people (how animals regard it is of course

a matter of conjecture) it does have its proponents, including the Princeton University bioethicist Peter Singer.

> Who has not been at a social occasion disrupted by the household dog gripping the legs of a visitor and vigorously rubbing its penis against them? In private not everyone objects to being used by her or his dog in this way, and occasionally mutually satisfying activities may develop.
>
> —Peter Singer, review of *Dearest Pet* for
> the erotic online magazine *Nerve*

> I saw the goat the next day—it did not seem too upset, but it is difficult to tell.
>
> —Unidentified Constable in Humberside, England,
> after commuter train passengers witnessed
> a man having sex with the farm animal

bigorexia (aka "muscle dysmorphic disorder")

Preoccupation, especially among bodybuilders, with imaginary physical shortcomings. Just as *anorexics* look in the mirror and see a fat person, bigorexics, no matter how massive or chiseled, look in the mirror and see a ninety-eight-pound weakling.

bipolar disorder (aka "manic depression")

Widely diagnosed disorder in which the patient cycles between high-flying manic episodes and periods of crushing depression.

Black Dog, the

Winston Churchill's pet name for his prolonged fits of *depression*.

blindsight

Vague stare affected by celebrities trying to avoid contact with the public.

Apart from the pesky paparazzi, people did not intrude on [Jacqueline Kennedy Onassis's] privacy, except maybe to call out "Hi, Jackie" when they passed her, and some of them received a smile back, or a wave, as she kept on walking her fast walk, with her eyes raised just high enough to avoid eye contact, in the celebrity manner of seeing but not seeing called *blindsight*.

—Dominick Dunne, *Vanity Fair*

blues, the

1. State of sadness or melancholy; depression. 2. Style of music believed originated by African Americans lamenting life's frustrations and tragedies, most often associated with a I-IV-V chord progression over a twelve-bar framework.

I got the Weary Blues
And I can't be satisfied.

—Langston Hughes

Some people say that to play the blues, you have to understand pain.

—B. B. King

See also *human condition, kvetch.*

Bobbitt, Lorena

The aptly named Venezuelan-born housewife who cut off her husband's penis and threw it out of a moving car. After the penis was recovered and surgically reattached, Mrs. Bobbitt, who claimed that her husband had repeatedly raped her, was tried and acquitted of all criminal charges. Mr. Bobbitt, who sold the fateful knife to the highest bidder on eBay, went on to become a porn star, an ordained minister in the Universal Life Church, and a prison inmate in Nevada after a conviction for attempted grand larceny.

He punch me, he kick me, he torture me with the Marine techniques.

—Lorena Bobbitt, explaining why
she mutilated her husband

Wouldn't it be ironic if the Lorena Bobbitt trial had ended in a hung jury?

—Howard Ogden

body dysmorphic disorder
Preoccupation with an imagined defect in appearance.
See also *bigorexia, eating disorder, plastic surgery addiction.*

body-piercing
Popular form of *self-mutilation*, especially among young Americans, who have rings, rods, studs, and other objects surgically inserted for adornment and/or enhancement of sexual pleasure. Hence the piercing of nostrils, lips, tongues, navels, nipples, and genitalia, and the relatively recent practice of tongue splitting, which can result in a slight lisp.
See also *modern primitive.*

booing
Sound uttered by spectators to signify disappointment or contempt. For some reason, booing seems to be, if not more prevalent, then more virulent, in the mid-Atlantic states, especially in the cities of New York (home of the "Bronx cheer" and the "raspberry") and Philadelphia, where, it is said, "They boo Santa Claus."

boredom
Condition of mental weariness; dullness; monotony.

The two real problems in life are boredom and death.

—Saul Bellow

Dear World: I am leaving because I am bored. I feel I have lived long enough. I am leaving you with your worries in this sweet cesspool. Good luck.

—George Sanders, suicide note

See also *ennui.*

"born to lose"
Phrase self-styled outlaws have tattooed on their arms (more an attitude than a predisposition).

breakthrough (rare)
A spurt of psycho-therapeutic progress.

bridezilla
Wedding consultants' name for a beastly bride-to-be so determined to make her wedding "perfect" that she'll destroy anything or anyone standing in her way.

broadcast bonhomie
Cloying geniality of celebrities on talk shows plugging their latest movie, book, or CD that may be engendered by the prospect of monetary gain or may simply be a function of innate phoniness.

Brooks, Albert (né Albert Einstein, 1947–)
Tortured, insecure Jewish actor, comedian, and director (including *Real Life* [1978] and *Modern Romance* [1981]) known as "The West Coast Woody Allen."

Brothers, Joyce (Joyce Diane Bauer Brothers, 1928–)
Deadpan TV shrink (aka "the mother of all media psychologists") who doesn't actually give advice, but rather purveys psychological research, usually prefacing her pronouncements with "*studies* show."

Bruce, Lenny (Leonard Alfred Schneider, 1926–1966)

Prototype "sick comedian" who died of a drug overdose at the age of forty while embroiled in a series of lawsuits and prosecutions for obscenity and drug possession. An iconoclastic social commentator, he both shocked and delighted conservative post–World War II audiences and profoundly influenced succeeding generations of comedians.

> People should be taught what is, not what should be. All my humor is based on destruction and despair. If the whole world were tranquil, without disease and violence, I'd be standing in the breadline—right back of J. Edgar Hoover.
> —Lenny Bruce, *The Essential Lenny Bruce* (1967)

Bubba eruption

See *Clinton, William Jefferson.*

burnout

Stress reaction to occupational demands that may manifest as fatigue, *depression, insomnia,* or substance abuse. Police officers, teachers, and medical professionals are particularly susceptible. See also *nervous breakdown.*

buzz

Pleasurable sensation, often artificially self-induced. According to UCLA psychopharmacologist Ronald K. Siegel, the human need for intoxication is actually a fourth drive, as powerful as hunger, thirst, or sexual desire, hence the craving for a *buzz* is inescapable.

> The desire to be fucked up probably leaves you, but the desire to be high probably never does.
> —Kris Kristofferson, *Esquire,* January 2004

bystander effect
Phenomenon documented by social scientists in which people are less likely to help someone in distress when there are others present who can also render assistance.

C

Camus, Albert (1913–1960)
French writer and philosopher of *the Absurd* whose characters, in such works as *The Stranger* (1942), *The Plague* (1947), *The Myth of Sisyphus* (1942), and *The Fall* (1956), are aware of the meaninglessness of life but refuse to succumb to it. Camus won the 1957 Nobel Prize for literature. He died in a car crash at the age of forty-seven.

catalog-induced anxiety
The anguish of envy.

> Today anyone can peruse the specifics of millionairehood. Television obsessively documents the lavish lives of the wealthy and glamorous. This creates, for some, a condition that might be called catalog-induced anxiety. People can see, in agonizing detail, all the expensive things they will never possess. This may make what a typical person possesses seem insufficient, even if the person is one of the tens of millions of Americans living, by the standards of history, in unprecedented comfort and freedom.
> —Gregg Easterbrook, *The Progress Paradox: How Life Gets Better While People Feel Worse* (2003)

catastrophizing
The magnifying of a small problem into a big one when under stress.
See also *defensive pessimism*.

catch-22

Contradictory situation based on twisted logic; an absurd predicament, from Joseph Heller's novel, *Catch-22*.

> "You mean there's a catch?"
>
> "Sure there's a catch," Doc Daneeka replied. "Catch-22. Anyone who wants to get out of combat duty isn't really crazy."
>
> There was only one catch and that was Catch-22, which specified that a concern for one's own safety in the face of dangers that were real and immediate was the process of a rational mind.
>
> Orr was crazy and could be grounded. All he had to do was ask; and as soon as he did, he would no longer be crazy and would have to fly more missions. Orr would be crazy to fly more missions and sane if he didn't, but if he was sane he had to fly them. If he flew them he was crazy and didn't have to; but if he didn't want to he was sane and had to. Yossarian was moved very deeply by the absolute simplicity of this clause of Catch-22 and let out a respectful whistle.
>
> "That's some catch, that Catch-22," he observed.
>
> "It's the best there is," Doc Daneeka agreed.
>
> —Joseph Heller, *Catch-22* (1961)

cat test

Technique for gauging the efficacy of experimental tranquilizers: The drug passes the test if a cat dosed with it hangs limp when lifted by the nape of the neck.

catharsis

Greek for "purge," the supposedly therapeutic surfacing of repressed feelings and memories.

See also *repression*.

catharsis theory

Freud declared that expressing anger in comparatively harmless ways relieves psychological pressure, but current research indicates that venting anger only increases it. So much for pillow-punching.

> There is a school of thought that believes it is wonderfully healthy for people to let loose with whatever anger they harbor, in all its natural force. Miss Manners need hardly mention that this is not an etiquette school.
>
> —Miss Manners (Judith Martin)

celebriphilia

Pathological desire to have sex with a *celebrity*.
See also *groupie*.

celebrity

A famous person, or, in Daniel Boorstin's famous phrase, someone "well-known for his well-knownness."

> In a country where there is no royalty and where, post-Watergate, politicians are held in almost universal contempt, celebrity is next to Godliness. Indeed, we want to believe in celebrities for the same reason we want to believe in God: their omnipotence and invincibility, however illusory, hold out the promise that we, too, have a crack at immortality.
>
> —Frank Rich

> Under the terms of a success that entails the minting of the human personality into the coin of celebrity, the bargain has a Faustian component. Wittingly or unwittingly, the chosen individual becomes available to the public feast. The celebrity receives the gift of wealth and applause; in return the gossip

columnists and the writers of high-minded editorials can do
what they like with the carcass of his humanity.
—Lewis H. Lapham, *Money and Class in America* (1988)

In France, philosophers are celebrities. In the United States,
celebrities are philosophers.
—Peter Carlson, *The Washington Post*

Celebrities suffer from a kind of spiritual acceleration, as if,
having already arrived, they have no further use for patience.
—Anatole Broyard, *The New York Times Book Review*

celebrity sufferer
Famous person with a problem.

SEVEN STAGES OF CELEBRITY SUFFERING

1. Celebrity gets arrested/has breakdown/almost dies.

2. Celebrity serves time/enters rehab/gets religion.

3. Celebrity attributes troubles to some "disease."

4. Celebrity "goes public" to "help others."

5. Celebrity's disease is declared more common than previously
believed.

6. Celebrity's disease gets Web site.

7. Celebrity's disease gets tax-exempt status.

cell yell

Loud talking on cell phones in public places by people with the apparent *neurotic need* to invade their own privacy.

> Do we have to yell about the results of our colonoscopy in a Home Depot?
> > —Carol Page, founder of Cellmanners.com

> So many free minutes, so little time.
> > —Howard Ogden, *Pensamentoes, Volume II* (2003)

Chast, Roz (1955–)

Cartoon chronicler of middle-class neuroses whose work appears regularly in the *New Yorker.* Chast is as much writer as artist: Her copy-intensive panels with their childlike drawings in fine-line ink pen and watercolor wash often have titles as well as captions, a conceptual style dubbed "new narrative cartooning."

> The Tournament of Neuroses Parade
> [one of the floats is labeled, "I Never Really Broke Away from My Parents"]

> The Little Engine That Coulda Woulda Shoulda
> ("I knew I could, so why didn't I?")

> The Imperfect Hostess
> ("We're having DIRT for dinner! And you're not invited! I forgot your names, anyway.")

Her stock characters are scrawny, listless children, slouching nerds with shirt pocket pen-protectors, bald-headed, middle-aged men in checkered pants, and perm-coiffed women squinting through cat's-eye glasses. Her recurring theme is the anxiety of modern life, particularly the stresses of parenthood. Her morbid fascinations

include foliage, which she calls "kitsch in nature," the difference between concrete and cement, and her various phobias, including milk
("Milk Toast: One of the world's most deadly foods!"), automo-
biles (she didn't drive until her thirties), and exposed electrical wiring
(too much like the inside of a human body). She's also something
of a hypochondriac who's been known to complain of "fizzy fingers."

She lives in suburban Connecticut with her husband, the
short story writer Bill Franzen, and their two children.

> Roz never seems to finish a beverage—she always leaves a half
> inch in the bottom of the glass. I kept asking why, and she fi-
> nally admitted she's worried about residue. She's afraid it might
> be different down there.
> —Bill Franzen

chemically induced disability
Therapeutic euphemism for drug addiction.

childhood
The early stage of a person's existence during which the seeds of
neurosis are planted.

> A happy childhood, I've always believed, is the worst possible
> preparation for life.
> —Kinky Friedman

Christmas blues, the
Anxiety and depression affecting the estimated one in four persons overwhelmed by the physical, psychological, and financial
demands of the Christmas season.

> The black dog of Christmas . . .
> —Roger Angell, *The New Yorker,* December 22 & 29, 2003

Christmas is a holiday that persecutes the lonely, the frayed, and the rejected.

—Jimmy Cannon

Something in me resists the calendar expectation of happiness. *Merry Christmas yourself!* it mutters as it shapes a ghostly grin.

—J. B. Priestley, *Outcries and Asides* (1974)

chutzpah

Gall, impudence, audacity. Leo Rosten's *Joys of Yiddish* retails the classic example: "That quality which enables a man who has just murdered his mother and father to throw himself upon the mercy of the court as an orphan."

Former U.S. Vice President Spiro T. Agnew, who pleaded no contest to tax evasion and resigned in 1973 amid bribery charges, filed for a tax refund of $142,000, the sum he paid to Maryland as restitution on bribes he took as governor. (The request was denied as "ludicrous.")

The greatest political stylist the world has ever known was Mrs. Eva Perón. The crowning moment of her entire career was when she rose in her box in the opera house in Buenos Aires to make a speech. She lifted her hands to the crowd, and as she did so, with a sound like railway coaches in a siding, the diamond bracelets slid from her wrists to her armpits. When the expensive clatter had died away, her speech began, "We, the shirtless . . ."

—Quentin Crisp, *How to Have a Life-Style* (1978)

Cioran, Emil M. (1911–1995)

Romanian novelist, essayist, aphorist, and *ennuyé*, variously dubbed a "connoisseur of despair," a "cosmic comedian," and "the last worthy disciple of Nietzsche." A self-described "skeptic-on-duty in a decaying world," his subjects are solitude, absurdity, the agony of consciousness, boredom, alienation, and his own misanthropy. "I anticipated in my lifetime the disappearance of our species. But the gods have been against me."

Cioran was born in Transylvania, the son of a Romanian Orthodox priest. He described an idyllic childhood, with freedom to do as he pleased, which meant associating with town drunks and playing in a cemetery (in later life he would go to cemeteries to cheer himself up). His world collapsed, he said, when his family moved to a larger town. He studied literature and philosophy at Bucharest University, then went to Paris on a scholarship in 1937. He remained there for the rest of his life, living reclusively in a Left Bank apartment as a self-described "parasite."

It has been said that Cioran searched for "hard answers to impossible questions" in the tradition of the great French aphorists La Rochefoucauld, Chamfort, and Valéry. Indeed, his elegant aphorisms deal with the essential problems of the *human condition:* birth, death, faith, and despair. He is gloomy and pessimistic, yet his mind is so supple and his prose so pungent that he tends to uplift rather than depress, and over the last few decades he has become a cult figure in the West.

Cioran wrote in French, but most of his books have been translated into English by the Pulitzer Prize–winning poet Richard Howard. That he was "obsessed with the worst" is reflected in the titles: *On the Heights of Despair* (1992), *Syllogisms of Bitterness* (1952), *All Gall Is Divided* (1980), *The Temptation to Exist* (1968), *The Trouble with Being Born* (1976), *A Short History of Decay* (1975), and *Drawn and Quartered* (1983; one of the chapter titles: "Stabs at Bewilderment"). His friend and fellow Paris exile Samuel Beckett, who paid Cioran's rent and introduced him to English-speaking readers through the *Evergreen Review*, wrote of him, "He is not a writer of despair, there is always a little blue light."

I sought in doubt a remedy for anxiety. The cure ended by making common cause with the disease.

—E. M. Cioran, *The Trouble with Being Born* (1976)

cleanliness compulsion

The driving need to keep oneself and one's surrounding clean, often coupled with fear of germs.

> I clean my own house often. I clean secretly. When I am talking on the phone, sharing gossip, one hand is stirring the toilet brush. I may be scouring the stovetop as my friend tells me of her breakup. I may be fingering the dust off baseboards at the moment another friend confesses her affair. I am interested in their stories, but the moving of dirt helps me process the information. In the midst of entropy, of the decay of life and love, there is security in a polished mirror. I may not see myself clearly, but I won't see spattered toothpaste, either.
>
> —Louise Rafkin, *Other People's Dirt* (1998)

> When [Joe Ancis] would leave the house he would take a bar of soap with him in his pocket, so that if he had to go to the men's room somewhere, he could scrub up. (You can't possibly urinate without washing your hands immediately afterwards!) And using the soap in the men's room was absolutely out of the question. Liquid soap was all right. This he would look for, pray for, but if there was no liquid soap, he would have to go for his own bar of emergency soap. Take that Ivory out, wash the hands good, then paper towels; if no paper towels, go for some toilet paper. Never use the roll of cloth towels in those machines that always get stuck. When you're finally through with this surgical scrub-up job, clean, immaculate, not a germ crawling on your hands, then what are you going to do? Turn around and open that dirty door with all the filth on the doorknob? You'd blow the whole job. No, reach in your pocket, glove your hand in the lining of the pocket, then with a practiced little twist, pop the door open and slip out. Safe!
>
> —Albert Goldman,
> *Ladies and Gentlemen, Lenny Bruce!!!* (1974)

I'm always on the lookout for dust in secret places where I
haven't looked before to see if some has landed there. If I see it,
I can't stop thinking about it until I get rid of it.

—Isabella Rossellini

See also *anal retentive personality.*

Clinton, William Jefferson (1946–) (aka "Slick Willy," "Bubba")

The forty-second President of the United States, the second
president in history to be impeached, and perhaps the most intricate personality to occupy the White House since *Richard
Nixon:* the lying, the *sex addiction,* the shameless pardons, the
cheating at golf, his periodic lapses have come to be known as
Bubba eruptions, and the adjective "Clintonian" has come to signify mendacious parsing: during grand jury testimony he de-
fended previous statements about his affair with former White
House intern Monica Lewinsky by quibbling over the precise
definition of his words, uttering the now famous statement, "It
depends on what the meaning of the word 'is' is" and claiming
that "sexual relations" did not to him mean "sexual intercourse."

Clinton's behavior is truly Nixonian. And it is worse in one way.
Nixon's actions, however neurotic and criminal, were motivated
by and connected to the exercise of presidential power. He knew
the place he occupied, and he was determined not to give it up
to those he regarded as "enemies." Clinton acted—and still, even
in his supposed mea culpa, acts—as if he does not recognize
what it means to be president of the United States.

—David Broder, *The Washington Post,* August 19, 1998

Did Clinton actually think that he could get blow jobs from a
Jewish woman and there would be no *consequences?*

—Larry David

closure
Final resolution or conclusion. In its popular sense, closure represents the simplistic notion that grief can be resolved—"put behind us"—through some sort of climactic event or gesture. Closure was elevated to Holy Grail status by the mass media and politicians in the aftermath of the Oklahoma City bombing and the 9/11 attacks. In one instance, an anonymous medical technician from Queens, New York, asked by a reporter why he was getting a 9/11 memorial tattoo, shrugged and replied, "I don't know, closure?"

clutter buddy
The burgeoning "clutter management" movement has produced the clutter buddy, a recovering clutterer (formerly "pack rat") who supports someone actively obsessed with the accumulation of unnecessary objects, and "clutter clinics" where clutterers learn to avoid such pitfalls as "churning," the movement of clutter from one place to another instead of throwing it away.

codependent (formerly "unselfish")
Originally used to describe the spouses and close associates of alcoholics, it now signifies the desire to help and support another person at the expense of one's own *happiness.* Melody Beattie's 1986 bestseller *Codependent No More* made it a household word and generated countless *support groups* for codependents, which may be a contradiction in terms.

> You're told to like the group things and not disagree with the group, [but] in actuality, they're replicating the way codependence evolved. A lot of these people came from families where they were taught not to think for themselves and . . . the treatment is the worst thing they could be doing.
> —Marc Kern, clinical psychologist

See also *people pleaser.*

cognitive dissonance

Theory first proposed by American psychologist Leon Festinger in 1957 based on the idea that people are uncomfortable with inconsistencies in their beliefs. Santa Claus is for many children their first experience of cognitive dissonance: They're told he's one individual living at the North Pole with "Mrs. Claus" and "the elves," yet at Christmastime they see multiple Santas on street corners. Of course, it eventually dawns on them that Santa's a myth, but if they're lucky, no one actually tells them he doesn't exist. The classic example of cognitive dissonance is the Goofy/Pluto dichotomy: The two Disney characters are both dogs, yet Goofy talks (albeit, well, goofily), wears human clothing, and even drives a car, while Pluto is a real dog who wears no clothes, doesn't talk, and wags his tail. What's that about?

collapse anxiety

Gnawing fear that the United States is heading for a fall.

> Deep-seated in the minds of many is a fear that the West cannot sustain its current elevated living standards and liberty. We fear the economy will collapse, or natural resources will run out. We fear that the West's military bulwark will be neutralized by some genetically engineered bio-horror; that terrorism or environmental calamity will overwhelm societies based on openness and plenty. Collapse anxiety is essential to understanding why Americans do not seem more pleased with the bounty that most of us enjoy—and this anxiety was in our minds well before September 11, 2001, when the physical collapse of the twin towers made tangible an inner fear.
> —Gregg Easterbrook, *The Progress Paradox: How Life Gets Better While People Feel Worse* (2003)

comb-over

Male effort to cover an obvious bald spot by draping lengths of hair or brushing it forward. Though popular, the comb-over is ultimately self-defeating because the attempt to hide a bald spot only makes it more conspicuous. Notable comb-overers: Julius Caesar, Napoleon Bonaparte, General Douglas MacArthur, Rudy Giuliani (formerly), *Donald Trump* (more of a nest, really), Tony Kornheiser (strand-over), and Zero Mostel as Max Bialystock in the first movie version of *The Producers* (1968).

> The method preferred by most balding men for making themselves look silly is called the "comb-over" which is when a man grows the hair on one side of his head very long and combs it across the bald area, creating an effect that looks like an egg in the grasp of a large tropical spider.
>
> —Dave Barry

See also *denial*.

comfort food (formerly "home cookin' ")

Simple foods, often childhood favorites mothers cooked for their children, that alter brain chemistry to provide soothing relief from stress. Most comfort food is high in mood-elevating sugar, satisfying fat, or both. According to a *study* at the University of Illinois, the top four comfort foods are potato chips, ice cream, cookies, and candy, but homemade standbys are also deemed therapeutic, including meatloaf and mashed potatoes, pot roast, macaroni and cheese, tomato soup, and green bean casserole (green beans, canned onions, canned mushroom soup).

> Any food that makes you feel good is bad for you.
>
> —Gary Null

coming out (of the closet)
Process of announcing one's homosexuality to the world.

> It wasn't easy telling my family that I'm gay. I made my carefully
> worded announcement at Thanksgiving. It was very Norman
> Rockwell. I said, "Mom, would you please pass the gravy to a
> homosexual?" She passed it to my father. A terrible scene fol-
> lowed.
>
> —Bob Smith

commitment
Act of pledging oneself emotionally to another person. In
American society, young women complain of young men's aversion to permanent relationships, and some actually contend that
men who can't commit suffer from an unrecognized but wide-
spread form of *attention-deficit disorder*.

commitment phobe
One with a pathological fear of *commitment*.

common sense
Instinctive good judgment. Sadly, it is regarded a quaint notion
that the shoals of life can be successfully navigated with the
sturdy rudder of nonacademic wisdom.
See also *intellectual boob*.

communication
According to conventional wisdom, the sine qua non of a
healthy *relationship*, but see *self-delusion*.

compassion fatigue
1. Form of *burnout* experienced by members of the "helping
professions" (doctors, nurses, social workers, police, firefighters)
characterized by physical, emotional, and spiritual exhaustion.

2. Public numbness to tragedy as a consequence of saturation media coverage of wars, epidemics, natural disasters, etc. See also *information sickness.*

compassionate inaccuracy

Politically correct practice of doctoring scores to make losers feel better about themselves. In 1999, high school hockey coaches in Boston admitted to having systematically changed the scores of lopsided games they reported to local newspapers to avoid damaging the *self-esteem* of the losing teams (thereby giving new meaning to the term "point shaving").

compulsive overeating (formerly "gluttony")

See *eating disorder.*

compulsive gambler (formerly "degenerate gambler")

One who gambles to *self-destructive* excess.

> I always had one ear offstage, listening for the call from the bookie.
>
> —Walter Matthau

> Gambling was a kind of therapy that cut through all the affectations and reduced everything to basic naked aggression.
>
> —Neal Gabler, *An Empire of Their Own* (1988)

> *God is a fuckin' faggot!*
>
> —John Gotti, on learning he had lost $20,000 on a baseball game

compulsive shopping disorder

Binge buying leading to financial hardship and feelings of guilt. According to a Stanford University study published in the *Journal of Clinical Psychiatry,* the antidepressant citalopram is effective in curbing the overwhelming urge to shop. Skeptics, however, see the findings, from a trial involving only twenty-four subjects, as an instance of a disturbing trend: drug companies promoting the redefinition of normal behavior as "compulsive" to promote sales.

> Compulsive shopping is a very rare condition, but if it's defined liberally enough it could encompass millions of people who like to shop. Just because people shop a lot and are distressed by it doesn't necessarily mean it's a disorder.
>
> —Allan Horwitz,
> Rutgers University professor of sociology,
> *Knight Ridder Tribune Business News,* August 1, 2003

See also *pharmacracy state, retail therapy.*

conduct disorder
Psychobabble for "juvenile delinquency."

confabulation
Filling in memory gaps with fabricated stories, a common form of *self-delusion.*

> The Swiss psychologist Jean Piaget once told an interviewer about one of his first conscious experiences. He remembered being pushed in a perambulator by his nanny when she was attacked by a man who wanted her purse. Throughout his youth Piaget recalled the attacker's bearded face, the nanny screaming and scratching his arm, the flash of sun on her parasol as she beat him with it, and other tightly focused details. Later in life, as a young adult, he discovered that the incident he remembered so vividly had never happened. The nanny had been

unaccountably late getting the little boy home and had concocted the tale of the attacker to satisfy his parents. Evidently she was a good storyteller, and little Piaget soaked it up. Retellings by his parents no doubt further strengthened the details in his memory. His nanny's false alibi became absolute truth to him.

—John Daniel, "The Province of Personal Narrative"

confrontainment
TV shows in which ordinary people confront each other with festering grievances, as when a wife assails her husband for his affair with a transsexual teamster, or a daughter reveals to her mother that she would rather go to school than work as a prostitute in order to help Mom buy crack.

consciousness
Awareness of one's own identity, thoughts, and feelings, perhaps the one trait distinguishing humans from animals, and the sine qua non of *neurosis*.

The world begins and ends with us. Only our consciousness exists, it is everything, and this everything vanishes with it.
—E. M. Cioran, *Anathemas and Admirations* (1991)

Consciousness isn't like a light switch that goes on or off. It's more like a dimmer on a light.
—Nathan Cope, anthropologist

Consciousness is a disease.
—Miguel de Unamuno

conspicuous austerity (aka "reduced consumerism")
Term coined by Joan Kron in her book *Home-Psych* (1983) to describe the practice of buying expensive goods and services that

appear simple or inexpensive, i.e., the studied attempt to appear less affluent while in fact sacrificing nothing.

constant whitewater
Relentless turbulence of modern corporate life in an era of globalization, cutbacks, downsizing, and restructuring.

control freak
Some degree of control over one's life is necessary for good physical and emotional health, but control freaks cross the line. In a futile attempt to control the world, they use a variety of methods from shouting, nagging, and withholding affection, to giving expensive gifts and feigning friendship. Deep down they fear criticism for their mistakes and believe that keeping control will allow them to avoid it. [Compiler's note: Or so they say. I personally dislike the term "control freak." I prefer "master and commander." JW]

> I used to be embarrassed and defensive when people accused me of being a control freak, but now, I say of course I want utter and complete control over every product I do. The audience buys my work because I do control it, because I am a perfectionist, because I care deeply.
>
> —Barbra Streisand,
> *Chicago Tribune*, November 19, 1996

> For our interview she [Barbra Streisand] personally hired the director, supervised the lighting, fixed the camera angles, and organized the flowers. She would have had time to grow them because she kept us waiting for five hours without a sign of apology.
>
> —Clive James

I never took drugs, because I was afraid. I'm a director, therefore I'm a control freak. I was afraid if I experimented with any kind of drugs or alcohol, I would lose control, and therefore I would never become a director.

—Steven Spielberg, *New York Daily News*, July 1998

I am a control freak. I am a perfectionist. But I'm trying to portray specific kinds of ideas. I'm trying to portray the best of what I can do. I want to be a teacher of the best things.

—Martha Stewart,
CBS News with Bryant Gumbel, March 1998

When I fly in a helicopter, I insist there be two sets of controls, one for me in case something happens to the pilot. I'm no expert, but I know enough to at least get the thing on the ground. Nothing scares me like the thought of not being in control.

—Jack Nicklaus, *Golf Digest*, April 2004

The last thing that I've been unable to control in my quest to control everything around me is death.

—Lars Ulrich, drummer, Metallica

counseling
General term for various forms of talk therapy in which a counselor offers guidance to a patient.

country music
More than any other popular music category, country songs are anthems to *neurotic* relationships and *dysfunctional* families, as evidenced by a sampling of titles.

"She's Actin' Single and I'm Drinkin' Doubles"

"When Your Phone Don't Ring You'll Know It's Me"

"I Bought the Shoes That Just Walked Out on Me"

"You're the Reason Our Kids Are So Ugly"

"How Can I Miss You If You Won't Go Away?"

"My Wife Ran Off with My Best Friend and I Sure Do Miss Him"

"I'm Comin' Back to You, One Barstool at a Time"

"Let's Do Something Cheap and Superficial"

"I've Been Flushed from the Bathroom of Your Heart"

"Thank God and Greyhound She's Gone"

"I Fell in a Pile of You and Got Love All Over Me"

"Get Your Tongue Out of My Mouth, Because I'm Kissing You Good bye."

crazy
Technically, mad or insane; colloquially, wildly or intensely passionate, obsessed, infatuated.

We're surrounded by crazy people.

—Tony Bill

I've always been crazy, but it's kept me from going insane.

—Waylon Jennings

If you ain't crazy, there's something wrong with you.

—Willie Nelson

A crazy person doesn't really lose his mind. It just becomes something more entertaining.

—George Carlin

creativity-equals-craziness equation
Romantic notion that creativity is a product of *repression* and that great artists are likely to be mentally unbalanced.

[The] "creativity equals craziness" equation . . . posits that all true artists are depressed and addicted to something more dangerous than the smell of Windex. I maintain that you can be simultaneously creative *and* compulsive. I have to.

—Louise Rafkin, *Other People's Dirt* (1998)

To be mad is not necessarily to be creative, or there'd be a Shelley on every corner.

—Anonymous Editorial,
The New York Times, October 15, 1993

creep defense
Sexual assault defense strategy to the effect that any woman who dates a man known to be sexually aggressive assumes the sexual risk and therefore deserves what she gets, up to and including rape. A new low in the blame-the-victim trend, the *creep defense* was employed on behalf of former heavyweight boxing champion Mike Tyson in his 1992 trial for rape and deviant conduct. See also *Twinkie defense.*

cross-dresser
One who wears clothing of the opposite sex as part of a fetish, a disguise, or for personal entertainment.
See also *in drab, in drag, transvestite.*

cult
Exclusive group of people who share an esoteric interest.

> A cult is a religion with no political power.
>
> —Tom Wolfe

cultural relativism
View that human behavior cannot be evaluated without reference to cultural context, and that one culture is never superior or inferior to another.

Curb Your Enthusiasm
See *David, Larry.*

cyberchondria
Hypochondria resulting from seeing one's symptoms on a medical Web site.

cynicism
Scornful, mocking, seen-it-all mentality.

> I worry [that] no matter how cynical you become, it's never enough to keep up.
>
> —Jane Wagner, *The Search for Signs of Intelligent Life in the Universe* (1986)

D

Dangerfield, Rodney (né Jacob Cohen, 1921–2004)
American comedian and actor whose signature lament, "I don't get no respect," fixed his name in the language as shorthand for someone or something ignored or disregarded.

NO RESPECT

I was such an ugly baby, my mother never breast fed me. She told me that she only liked me as a friend.

My father carries around the picture of the kid who came with his wallet.

I told my wife the truth. I told her I was seeing a psychiatrist. Then she told me the truth: that she was seeing a psychiatrist, two plumbers, and a bartender.

—Rodney Dangerfield

dark night of the soul, the
Godless despair; utter loneliness; from the title of a poem by the Christian mystic St. John of the Cross (1542–1591).

Sometimes I lie awake at night, and I ask, "Where have I gone wrong?" Then a voice says to me, "This is going to take more than one night."

—Charles M. Schulz
(Charlie Brown in *Peanuts* comic strip)

In a real dark night of the soul it is always three o'clock in the morning.

—F. Scott Fitzgerald, *The Crack-Up* (1945)

See also *absurd, abyss, angst, human condition.*

David, Larry (1947–)

[Compiler's note: I considered recusing myself from this entry on grounds of personal bias, because Larry David and I are so much alike it's scary: Like Larry, I'm a Jewish male born in 1947 who moved to Los Angeles from the East Coast and who finds daily life here an endless series of annoyances. Growing up in the 1950s and '60s, we both loved *The Phil Silvers Show* (see *I Knew It! syndrome*). During the '70s, we both joined the Army Reserve and wore short wigs over our long hair. We both received essentially worthless liberal arts degrees from large, mediocre, mid-Atlantic universities. We're both health conscious and assiduous about personal hygiene (e.g., Larry and I both floss religiously), we both hate to travel, and neither of us can abide Disneyland. And, just like Larry, I play golf but derive no pleasure from it.

Spooky, no? No wonder his *persona* on *Curb Your Enthusiasm* unfailingly expresses my innermost thoughts and feelings. Which is why I briefly doubted my journalistic objectivity, but I finally decided that keen insight trumps detachment. JW]

Former standup comedian and *Seinfeld* cocreator, and the model for the character of George Costanza who, David says, is more like him than he is. He oversaw the first six seasons of *Seinfeld* and was periodically heard as the voice of George Steinbrenner. In 1996, after writing some sixty *Seinfeld* episodes filled with characters and incidents from his own life (his avowed guiding principle was "no hugging, no learning"), he quit, citing the overwhelming pressures of running the top comedy show on television. He returned two years later to write the final episode in which Jerry, George, Elaine, and Kramer end up in jail for being bad people. He is reputed to have earned $200 million from syndication rights.

After his feature film, *Sour Grapes* (1998), was a critical and commercial disappointment, he returned to television in the year 2000 with the ironically titled HBO comedy series *Curb Your Enthusiasm*, which has been hailed as one the funniest in the history of the medium. The critic Tom Shales proclaimed Larry a "comic genius," and it is no exaggeration: First with *Seinfeld* and then with *Curb Your Enthusiasm*, he has created a new comedy genre: Postmodern Jewish Humor.

In *Curb Your Enthusiasm*, Larry plays Larry David, a man very much like himself: Both have identical histories, drive the same car, live in the same part of town, and have the same friends. *Curb* is shot faux cinéma vérité, unrehearsed and unscripted, with no studio audience and no laugh track. The actors improvise much of their dialogue from a basic outline, and only Larry knows the intricate plots, in which innocent miscommunications and petty deceptions result in perverse comeuppance for Larry. His friends appear as themselves, including Jason Alexander, Julia Louis-Dreyfus, Kathy Griffin, Mary Steenburgen, Ted Danson, Martin Short, and *Richard Lewis*, whom Larry met at summer camp when they were twelve. (They've apparently been yelling at each other ever since.)

Larry's *Curb Your Enthusiasm* character, whom critics have called "self-absorbed," "duplicitous," "irritable," "abrasive," "argumentative," "an unhappy, insecure jerk," "a prickly pessimist," "a lanky misanthrope," and a "copacetic sourball," is perhaps the most misunderstood *persona* on television. To set the record straight, the *Curb* "Larry" does *not* have an inordinate sense of entitlement, and he is *not* hypersensitive to petty slights. If he's perpetually disgruntled, it's because there's so much to be disgruntled about. If he alienates people, it's usually *their* fault. He isn't rude, he's direct. Inevitably, things are taken the wrong way, as when a lesbian receptionist is offended when "Larry" suggests that she and her partner name their adopted Chinese baby "Tang." ("It's a juice," "Larry" says, "but it has Chinese overtones.") And when he tells a man who's shaved his head, "We don't consider you part of the bald community," he isn't trying to *offend*, it's just his sense of justice talking, because "Larry" is always true to his personal code, no matter the consequences. If he demands competence and civility from members of the service class (waiters, salesmen, and parking-lot attendants seem to have it in for him), if he's vexed by long waits at the pharmacy or the doctor's office and has the temerity to *complain*, does that make him a bad guy? It isn't easy getting through the day, even for someone worth a couple hundred million bucks. Why waste time on "stop-and-chats" with casual acquaintances? Why leave a perfectly good restaurant after a meal and go to *another* restaurant for dessert? Why thank *both* husband and wife for buying dinner when the wife has never worked a day in her life? Why let some arrogant network suit get away with stealing your takeout shrimp? Why *not* argue with children when they're wrong? How else are they going to learn?

Does "Larry" occasionally lose his temper? Of course, but not without justification. (As a standup the real Larry would sometimes throw down the microphone and storm off the stage when an audience displeased him, but that was *their* fault.) If "Larry" occasionally bends the truth (okay, he lies *a lot*) it's only because there are so many delicate situations out there, and he only fibs to make life easier for others (okay, *himself*). Some say he's Quixotic, but I say he's a crusader against life's small injustices. He fights the little battles most people deem futile or self-defeating. He fights the good fight against, well, *inconvenience*. Isn't that just as important, in its way, as battling tyranny and hunger? Isn't *that* a kind of heroism?

> I would say that knowing George, you know more about me than you do if you speak to me. Because I feel like I'm the

phony, I'm the fake. People who are talking to me, they're not
getting sincerity, for the most part. They're getting something,
they're getting politeness, they're getting a nice person, but it's
not real. I think George is much more real than I am.

—Larry David, "The Power of Self-Loathing"
by David Noonan, *The New York Times Magazine*,
April 12, 1998

The person on the show [*Curb Your Enthusiasm*] actually has
more character than I do. He's not as bright, but inside, he has
more character. I'd rather be the person on the show.

—Larry David, *Esquire*, March 2002

I think you can make a much better assessment of who a person
is by what you're seeing on screen than by what you're seeing in
life. . . . On the show, I can say the things I think about, which I
can't say in life. I can get into arguments that I wouldn't get into.
You can't do anything in life. Other than golf, it's very restrictive. The social barriers in life are so intense and horrific that
every encounter is just fraught with so many problems and
dread. Every social situation is a potential nightmare.

—Larry David, *Entertainment Weekly*,
September 20, 2002

Every relationship is just so tenuous and precarious. One tiny
miscommunication or mistake and it could be all over. I'm talking about siblings! A Thanksgiving thing that somehow goes
wrong—bringing the wrong dish—all of a sudden, sisters aren't
talking after forty-five years!

—Larry David, *The New Yorker*, January 19, 2004

He's a brilliant curmudgeon who pursues his notions of justice
with far more fervor than sense. He becomes outraged when

people tell lies, even small ones, like saying their sweaters are 100 percent cashmere. Yet he automatically lies rather than face an embarrassing situation. He's ridiculous and recognizable and strangely endearing.

—Julie Salamon, *The New York Times,* September 30, 2001

Larry gets to his neuroses not from a Method school—he's the Olivier of neurosis. I don't think in real life he suffers that much internally. I hope not. His obsessiveness is to make good art and be a good father and husband. I *think.* I say that about people, and then you read the next day that someone was dressed up like Peter Pan on top of a bicycle.

—Richard Lewis, *Esquire,* March 2002

Whenever Larry [on *Curb Your Enthusiasm*] tries to apologize, tries to be a better person, the injured party ingraciously dumps on him, gets carried away with indignation and turns self-righteous, petty, and crazily vengeful. It's as if Larry is eternally lashed to some great karmic wheel, taking punishment that is spectacularly out-of-proportion to his crimes. He's repeatedly thwarted in his attempts to do the right thing by one immutable fact of life: other people.

—Joyce Millman, Salon.com, October 9, 2000

You've seen one sunset, you've seen them all.

—Larry David, quoted by Mary Steenburgen

defense mechanism
According to Freud, the psyche protects itself by unconsciously blotting out unpleasant feelings or thoughts, specifically by means of *rationalization, repression, sublimation,* or *denial.*

defensiveness

Tendency to resist criticism in order to protect the *ego*.

TIP: If you want to befuddle someone in an argument, accuse them of being "defensive." Either their silence will win you the argument by default, or their denial will confirm the accusation.

defensive pessimism

According to psychologist Julie Norem, positive thinking doesn't work for some people, who should try defensive pessimism. Here's how it works: In the face of an anxiety-producing task (a public speech, say) instead of psyching yourself *up*, psych yourself *down* by consciously lowering your expectations. Rehearse everything that could go wrong, and devise strategies to avert every conceivable glitch. This will produce a sense of control, which will reduce anxiety and help you perform effectively. Or, maybe not.

> I survive by expecting the worst. . . . Without my delight in adversity and the prospect of defeat, I would have gone under years ago.
> —Russell Baker, *Chicago Tribune*, July 26, 1988

See also *catastrophizing, optimism/pessimism*.

delusion

False belief or opinion held in the face of evidence to the contrary.

> Delusion, n. The father of a most respectable family, comprising Enthusiasm, Affection, Self-denial, Faith, Hope, Charity, and many other goodly sons and daughters.
> —Ambrose Bierce, *The Devil's Dictionary* (1911)

Delusion: belief said to be false by someone who does not share it.
> —Thomas Szasz, *The Untamed Tongue* (1990)

See also *delusions of grandeur, Othello delusion.*

delusions of grandeur
Irrational belief that one is a great or powerful person.

Delusions of grandeur make me feel a lot better about myself.
> —Jane Wagner, *The Search for Signs of Intelligent Life in the Universe* (1986; performed by Lily Tomlin)

I'm a highly, highly, highly creative human being.
> —Kim Basinger

I'm making a conscious decision to take this whole Judaism thing seriously. I think the Jews need me right now.
> —Geraldo Rivera, on plans to marry his fifth wife in a synagogue (2003)

See also *narcissism.*

demons
Figuratively, persistent inner torment; also, a device for excusing bad behavior or avoiding responsibility for one's actions, e.g., sometimes we're able to "exorcise" our demons, but sometimes they get the best of us.

The Devil made me do it.
> —Flip Wilson (as Geraldine on *Rowan and Martin's Laugh-In,* 1968–73)

demonstrative

Given to open display of affection. Not the first word that comes to mind when describing American males.

> If you weren't my son, I'd hug you.
> —Hank Hill (Mike Judge), *King of the Hill*

denarration

Term coined by novelist-culture critic Douglas Coupland to describe the emptiness of modern life:

> One factor that sets us apart from all other animals is that our lives need to be stories—narratives—and that when our stories vanish we feel lost, dangerous, out of control and susceptible to the forces of randomness. I call the process whereby one loses one's life story "denarration."
>
> Denarration is the technical way of saying "not having a life."
> "Brad doesn't have a life"; "Brad is denarrated."
>
> Until recently, culture provided us with all the components essential for the forging of identity. These components included: religion, family, ideology, class strata, geography, politics, and a sense of living within a historic continuum.
>
> Suddenly . . . with the deluge of electronic and information media, these stencils within which we trace our lives began to vanish. . . . It became possible to be alive yet have no religion, no family connections, no ideology, no sense of class location, no politics, and no sense of history. Denarrated.
> —Douglas Coupland, *The New Republic*, December 12, 1994

See also *information sickness*.

denial

Unconscious *defense mechanism* that numbs anxiety by refusing to acknowledge unpleasant realities, thoughts, or feelings. It is believed that the stress of maintaining denial can suppress the immune system and trigger such complications as *eating disorders* and heart problems, and in extreme cases may even cause psychosis. How to rid oneself of pernicious denial? There's the rub: When you're in denial you don't know it, and if you don't know you're in it, how can you get out of it?

> Never underestimate the power of denial.
> —Wes Bently in *American Beauty*
> (1999; screenplay by Alan Ball)

> In Los Angeles, there's a hotline for people in denial. So far no one has called.
> —George Carlin

> The late psychologist Ernest Becker won the 1974 Pulitzer Prize for his book *The Denial of Death* (1973), and wrote that without denial, human beings might become paralyzed by fear on their way to work, frozen on a corner awaiting "the suction of the infinite"—and then never even make it to Dunkin' Donuts.
> —Alex Kuczynski, *The New York Times,* July 28, 2002

> Individually, I am unhappy. I deny I am to myself; I deny I am denying anything to myself and to others. They must do the same. I must collude with their denial and collusion and they must collude with mine. So we are a happy family and we have no secrets from one another. If we are unhappy we have to keep it a secret and we are unhappy that we have to keep it a secret and unhappy that we have to keep secret the act that we have to keep it a secret and that we are keeping all that secret. But since we are a happy family you can see this difficulty does not arise.
> —R. D. Laing

What, me worry?
> —Alfred E. Neuman (emblem of *Mad* magazine)

depression (formerly "sadness")

Feelings of despair, hopelessness, *melancholy,* either as a mood or a symptom of a more serious condition. Depression has been called "the common cold of mental illness," and indeed, according to recent *studies,* more people see doctors for depression than for colds.

> The wittiest people are sometimes the most depressed: our prime satirists—think of S. J. Perelman or Dorothy Parker—are frequently nourished by dejection. As James Thurber wrote, "The little wheels of their invention are set in motion by the damp hand of melancholy."
>
> —Nora Sayre,
> Review of *The Letters of Nancy Mitford and Evelyn Waugh,*
> *The New York Times Book Review,* May 4, 1997

> By virtue of depression, we recall those misdeeds we buried in the depths of our memory. Depression exhumes our shames.
>
> —E. M. Cioran, *Anathemas and Admirations* (1991)

> In clinical depression, the psychological element merges into a chemical imbalance. Brain chemistry goes haywire, and when that happens it is catastrophic, an explosion of the mind, like the space shuttle *Challenger* going off in midair. Stress and anxiety have an effect on your brain's neurotransmitters, removing from your consciousness any ability to receive impulses of pleasure. A palpable shroud of melancholy descends on you and becomes a pain as severe as a crushed knee. You cannot bear living any longer. The act of daily living, the whole diurnal process, becomes such a struggle you want to get out of it.
>
> —William Styron, *Esquire,* December 1986

Diagnostic and Statistical Manual of Mental Disorders (DSM)
The American Psychiatric Association's official catalog of craziness, now in its fourth edition (DSM-IV), published in 1994. A DSM-IV diagnosis is generally required by insurance companies before they will pay for treatment.

The diagnostic manual does not refer to mental illness, only to mental disorders. It almost entirely is a description of behaviors and experiences, a style the American Psychiatric Association (APA) calls "etiologically neutral," meaning it does not deal with the causes. Actually, as a result of this neutrality, there is absolutely no medical validation, much less criteria, for the vast majority of mental disorders. An article discussing "conundrums" facing the Task Force on DSM-IV (authored by several members) in the *Journal of Abnormal Psychology* admits that, "unfortunately, in most instances," biological tests cannot be used even as "diagnostic indicators" since they are not specific to particular "mental disorders."

—Richard E. Vatz and Lee S. Weinberg,
USA Today Magazine, July 1993

It is worrisome that society is medicalizing more and more behavioral problems, often defining as addictions what earlier, sterner generations explained as weakness of will. Prodded by science, or what purports to be science, society is reclassifying what once were considered character flaws or moral failings as personality disorders akin to physical disabilities.

—George Will, *Newsweek,* November 25, 2002

There is still only one way to be sane—enjoy your friends, family, faith and job—but every year there are new ways to be crazy. Like the automobile industry, which once sold only sedans and station wagons but now offers endless variations on the SUV (including two versions of the Hummer), the

American Psychiatric Association now has an illness for almost every lifestyle. The current edition of its professional bible, the *Diagnostic and Statistical Manual of Mental Disorders IV,* contains—among scores of other diagnoses—a long list of specialized labels that was known in my grandmother's era as the jitters, including Attention-Deficit/Hyperactivity Disorder, Social Phobia, Panic Disorder with Agoraphobia, and Panic Disorder Without Agoraphobia.

—Walter Kirn, *Time* magazine, September 16, 2002

Psychiatrists themselves often acknowledge that the *Diagnostic and Statistical Manual of Mental Disorders* is increasingly arbitrary and unscientific. It also seems that the use of the term disorder, as opposed to disease or illness, is designed to fudge the question of whether these conditions have a biological basis.

—Jacob Sullum, *Reason,* July 2000

difficult

Euphemism for people who used to be called "temperamental" or "mean." The term is often applied to a performer who throws tantrums, is chronically late, unprepared, or just generally disagreeable. For example, by most accounts, operatic diva Kathleen Battle is the very avatar of *difficult.* In a classic anecdote, Ms. Battle is riding in a limousine when she decides she wants the driver to turn off the heat. Rather than stoop to communicate with him directly, she telephones her manager, who calls the opera house, which calls the livery service, which calls the driver, who turns off the heat. When it was announced in 1994 that she had been fired by the Metropolitan Opera after years of allegedly monstrous behavior, the staff literally applauded.

Other reputedly *difficult* performers: Kirk Douglas, Burt Lancaster, Katharine Hepburn (dubbed "Katharine of Arrogance" by crew members), Judy Garland, Peter Sellers, Maria Callas, Laurence Harvey, Jane Fonda, Brett Butler, Bruce Willis, Cybill Shepherd, Martin Lawrence, Dennis Hopper, John Travolta, Raquel Welch (who was reportedly fired from MGM's *Cannery Row* for taking three hours to put on makeup), Faye Dunaway, Diana Ross, Bette Midler, Alec Baldwin, Barbra Streisand (once described by a director as "a cross between Groucho Marx and a Sherman tank"), Steve McQueen, Val Kilmer, Burt Reynolds, and others.

I've got a lot of things to do, and I don't have time to be classified as *difficult*, and I don't have time to care.

—Kim Basinger,
of the $5 million breach of contract suit brought by the producers
of *Boxing Helena* after she dropped out of the picture

Until you're known in my business as a monster, you're not a *star*.

—Bette Davis

disillusionment
State of having lost one's illusions; disenchantment.

I stopped believing in Santa Claus when I was six. My mother took me to see him in a department store, and he asked for my autograph.

—Shirley Temple

We read the world wrong and say that it deceives us.

—Rabindranath Tagore, "Stray Birds"

Don't part with your illusions. When they are gone you may still exist, but you have ceased to live.

—Mark Twain

disorder
Ailment affecting the mind or body.

> Of all the countries on earth, we are the leader in disorders. The
> one most hung up on pathology. If we don't have attention-
> deficit disorder, we have one or another kind of personality dis-
> order. Or anxiety disorder. Or mood disorder. Other cultures
> just don't seem to have the problems we do. Or maybe they just
> don't have the psychiatrists and psychologists we do. . . . The en-
> tire premise of the therapeutic culture that pervades American
> life is summed up in that one word—disorder. There is some-
> thing wrong with us. We need to be diagnosed and treated. The
> corollary of this is that our problems—to the extent that they're
> actually problems—aren't part of our character. They're medical.
> Once it's put that way, we're off the hook. Nothing we can do
> about it, except see the doctor and take our pills.
>
> —Michael Skube,
> *The Atlanta Journal-Constitution,* March 24, 1998

divorce
Legal dissolution of marriage. In the United States, the divorce
rate is over 50 percent, higher for second marriages.

> Why leave the nut you got for one you don't know?
> —Loretta Lynn, *Esquire,* January 2002

> I've never been married, but I tell people I'm divorced so they
> won't think something's wrong with me.
>
> —Elayne Boosler

divorce jewelry
Baubles from a former marriage melted down and reworked into
new pieces. Women who have tried it say the melting process
yields a therapeutic thrill.

dog psychologist/psychiatrist
There it is: We live in a country in which dogs get psychotherapy.

domo (downwardly mobile)
Young professional who eschews a lucrative job in favor of lower-paying but more *meaningful* work.

doubt
Uncertainty; the state of being unsettled or unresolved, i.e., a signal quality of the *human condition*.

> Doubt is not a pleasant state of mind, but certainty is absurd.
> —Voltaire

> Man's most valuable trait is a judicious sense of what not to believe.
> —Euripides

> The fact that a believer is happier than a skeptic is no more to the point than the fact that a drunken man is happier than a sober one.
> —George Bernard Shaw

> The trouble with the world is that the stupid are cocksure and the intelligent are full of doubt.
> —Bertrand Russell

dread
To be in terror of; to anticipate with fear, distaste, or reluctance.

> I have a new philosophy. I'm only going to dread one day at a time.
> —Charles M. Schulz (Charlie Brown in *Peanuts*)

dream interpretation
Psychoanalytic technique based on *Freud*'s belief that unconscious wishes are revealed symbolically in dreams. Thus, for

example, staircases are seen to represent sexual intercourse (because you go up and down on them and wind up breathless—get it?).

The actor Tony Randall discovered that he and a friend, the lyricist Abe Burrows, had been seeing the same psychiatrist, and the two men decided to play a trick. They cooked up a fantastic dream with lots of bizarre details, and after rehearsing it thoroughly, Burrows recounted it to the therapist in his session on a Tuesday. Then Randall described the identical dream on the next Thursday, but when he finished, the shrink kept silent. No longer able to restrain himself, Randall finally asked, "Isn't there something unusual about what I just told you?" The psychiatrist thought for a moment and said, "Yes, as a matter of fact, there is: That was the third time this week I've heard that dream."

> Every dream reveals a psychological structure, full of significance.
>
> —Sigmund Freud

> They pick our dreams as though they were our pockets.
>
> —Karl Kraus, of psychoanalysts

> Interpreting dreams is like assaying static.
>
> —Howard Ogden, *Pensamentoes, Volume II* (2003)

drive-by hatred
Seemingly random acts of hostility perpetrated on total strangers, from threatening phone calls and vicious graffiti to Anthrax hoaxes.

DSM
See *Diagnostic and Statistical Manual of Mental Disorders.*

dysfunctional
Literally "functioning abnormally," *psychobabble* now applied not only to families and *relationships*, but also to countries, corporations, sports teams, and even pets.

> To err is dysfunctional, to forgive codependent.
> —Berton Averre

dysfunctional family (formerly "family")
A redundancy.

> Dysfunctional family: any family with more than one person in it.
> —Mary Karr, author of *The Liar's Club*

See also *family*.

E

eating disorder
Chronically abnormal eating habits such as binge eating, anorexia nervosa (intense fear of gaining weight coupled with *body dysmorphic disorder*), or bulimia nervosa (a cycle of binge eating and purging).

> I would lose ten or fifteen pounds in a week, eating nothing but cucumbers and working all day. My hands would shake all the time, and sometimes I'd pass out. But then I would go on these enormous binges. I lived alone and was very lonely. I made myself spaghetti dinners and chocolate cake and ate the whole thing, then tried to throw up because I was in such pain. But I couldn't. My body would be so swollen the

next day that it would hurt to touch, and my eyes would be little slits.

—Sally Field

Anorexia is just another word for nothing left to lose.

—Joy Behar

Eating is self-punishment; punish the food instead. Strangle a loaf of Italian bread. Throw darts at a cheesecake. Chain a lamb chop to the bed. Beat up a cookie.

—Gilda Radner

Gluttony is an emotional escape, a sign that something is eating us.

—Peter DeVries

It is harder to eat sparingly than to fast. Moderation requires awareness. Renunciation requires only the tyranny of will.

—Sandor McNab

eccentric

One who deviates from convention in an odd or whimsical way.

Eccentrics are misunderstood. . . . They aren't crazy. In fact, studying their adaptability can help neurotics. . . . Eccentrics and neurotics might be flamboyant and have obsessive hobbies. But to the eccentric, collecting is creative and joyful, while the neurotic knows no limits. Eccentrics are happier than most, visit doctors sixteen times less frequently, are healthier because of their optimism, maintain humor, and aren't stressed by conformity.

—Carol McGraw, *The Orange County Register*, January 23, 1996

ego

In Freudian psychology, the conscious part of the psyche as opposed to the *id* (base sexual urges) and the *superego* (moral conscience). In popular usage, the self-important constituent of the personality.

> If there's anything more important than my ego around, I want it caught and shot now.
>
> —Douglas Adams,
> *The Hitchhiker's Guide to the Galaxy* (1980)

> The ego is at once monstrous and fragile, like a balloon getting thinner as it inflates.
>
> —Howard Ogden, *Pensamentoes, Volume II* (2003)

> Alan, did you ever think you'd live so long that your prostate would be bigger than your ego?
>
> —Susie Essman to Alan King

> He was like a cock who thought the sun had risen to hear him crow.
>
> —George Eliot, *Adam Bede* (1859)

> I'm not handsome in the classical sense. The eyes droop, the mouth is crooked, the teeth aren't straight, the voice sounds like a Mafioso pallbearer, but somehow it all works.
>
> —Sylvester Stallone

> If I only had a little humility, I'd be perfect.
>
> —Ted Turner

emotion

Strong feelings such as joy, sorrow, love, or hate.

Athletes are often exhorted to "play with emotion," but

legendary football coach John McKay demurred: "It's overrated. My wife is emotional but she's a lousy football player."

> Ninety percent of our lives is governed by emotion. Our brains merely register and act upon what is telegraphed to them by our bodily experience. Intellect is to emotion as our clothes are to our bodies: we could not very well have civilized life without clothes, but we would be in a poor way if we had only clothes without bodies.
>
> —Alfred North Whitehead

> The energy that actually shapes the world springs from emotions.
> —George Orwell, "The Dilemma of the Intellectual"

> The advantage of the emotions is that they lead us astray.
> —Oscar Wilde

> The emotion may be endless. The more we express them, the more we may have to express.
> —G. K. Chesterton

emotional vulnerability
A strength that used to be a weakness.

empathy (formerly "sympathy")
Ability to understand and identify with another person's emotions.

> I feel your pain.
> —William Jefferson Clinton

> We're all the same schmuck.
> —Lenny Bruce

enabler
Rank *psychobabble* for one who helps another engage in *dysfunctional* behavior.

ennui
Extreme *boredom;* weariness; emptiness of spirit.

> While at Ambervale, to escape the "oppression of boredom," he walked over the hills to Chesterfield and found a dentist. "I described to him the symptoms, which I knew well, of an abscess.
>
> "He tapped a perfectly good tooth with his little mirror and I reacted in the correct way. 'Better have it out,' he advised.
>
> " 'Yes,' I said, 'but with ether.'
>
> "A few minutes' unconsciousness was like a holiday from the world. I had lost a good tooth, but the boredom was for a time dispersed."
>
> —Norman Sherry,
> *The Life of Graham Greene* (1989, 1994)

> One of ennui's most terrible components is the overwhelming feeling of ennui that comes over you whenever you try to explain it.
>
> —Ingmar Bergman, *From the Life of the Marionettes* (1980)

exhibitionist
One who derives sexual pleasure from exposing his or her privates to involuntary viewers.

> Momentary insanity, nothing more, nothing less.
>
> —Brandi Chastain, on why she tore off her shirt after scoring the
> winning goal in the 1999
> Women's World Cup soccer final

See also *flasher.*

exhaustion
Journalistic euphemism for a wide range of celebrity *disorders*, including nervous collapse, drug-induced dementia, and severe *stage fright*. *Exhaustion* is often used interchangeably with "dehydration," and in rare cases the two are used in tandem, as when comedian Martin Lawrence ran amok in a busy Los Angeles intersection in 1996. According to witnesses, he darted through traffic while babbling incoherently and gesticulating wildly at motorists, and upon arrest he was found to be carrying a handgun. After Lawrence was admitted to Cedars-Sinai, a "hospital spokesperson" described his condition as "exhaustion and dehydration."

F

factitious disorder
Physical or psychological *disorder* in which the symptoms are under the patient's control, such as in *Munchausen syndrome*.

false memory syndrome
Alleged "recollection," usually during *psychotherapy*, of childhood sexual abuse that never happened. *Freud* was a pioneer in the recovered memory field, prodding his patients to "recall" nonexistent sexual encounters with close relatives. According to the American Psychiatric Association, it is extremely rare for someone who was sexually abused as a child to forget it.

> We can easily distort memories for the details of an event that you did experience, and we can also go so far as to plant entirely false memories—we call them rich false memories because they are so detailed and so big.
> —Elizabeth Loftus, University of California, Irvine, psychologist, *The Guardian*, December 4, 2003

family, the
Beleaguered institution that can be a refuge from, or a cause of, psychological distress.

All happy families are alike; every unhappy family is unhappy in its own way.

—Leo Tolstoy,
Anna Karenina (1875)

When Tolstoy wrote that all happy families are alike, what he meant was that there are no happy families.

—Susan Cheever,
Treetops (1991)

To my way of thinking, the American family started to decline when parents began to communicate with their children.

—Erma Bombeck,
If Life Is a Bowl of Cherries—
What Am I Doing in the Pits? (1978)

Family dinners are more often than not an ordeal of nervous indigestion, preceded by hidden resentment and ennui and accompanied by psychosomatic jitters.

—M. F. K. Fisher

If Mr. Vincent Price were to be costarred with Miss Bette Davis in a story by Mr. Edgar Allan Poe directed by Mr. Roger Corman, it could not fully express the pent-up violence and depravity of a single day in the life of the average family.

—Quentin Crisp

When I can no longer bear to think of the victims of broken homes, I begin to think of the victims of intact ones.

—Peter DeVries, *The Tunnel of Love* (1954)

I'm sure Hitler was great with his family.

—George Carlin

fan behavior

In sports-crazed America, rooting has mutated into a broad
spectrum of behaviors, including infantile displays by drunken,
grotesquely costumed, face-painted fans in the seats and by
scantily clad, silicone-augmented, face-painted cheerleaders on
the sidelines. A disturbing recent trend is "synchronized fan behavior" like "the wave," or even more elaborate displays in which
spectators dress alike and root symbolically in unison, as when
the occupants of an entire section at a college basketball game
hold up newspapers while opposing players are being introduced
to signify their utter lack of interest.

During the telecast of Game Four of the 1984 NBA Cham-
pionship, the camera zoomed in on Ann-Margret in the stands.
The movie actress and erstwhile cheerleader glanced at the
camera, smiled, then looked straight ahead and joined the
crowd in chanting "GO, LAKERS; GO! GO, LAKERS, GO!"
Except she didn't just say "GO, LAKERS, GO!" She added a
contrapuntal "C'MON" on the beat between repetitions, so that
it was, "GO, LAKERS, GO! (C'MON!); GO, LAKERS, GO!
(C'MON!)."

fantasy (formerly "daydream")

Imagined event or dream that fulfills wishes or psychological
needs; a flight of fancy.

Fantasies are more than substitutes for unpleasant reality; they
are also dress rehearsals, plans. All acts performed in the world
begin in the imagination.

—Barbara Grizzuti Harrison, "Talking Dirty,"
Ms., October 1973

When I examine myself and my methods of thought, I come close to the conclusion that the gift of fantasy has meant more to me than my talent for absorbing positive knowledge.

—Albert Einstein

Fantasy is one of the soul's brightest porcelains.

—Pat Conroy, *Beach Music* (1995)

feelings

Feelings have found a home in America and their champion in *pop psychology*, for which feelings are better than thoughts. Hence you are exhorted to "get in touch with your feelings" and to "do what feels right" and to "go with your gut."

> Today's America is awash in expressed feelings. As a result of the tremendous successes in the practice of pop psychology and junk science, "feeling" is now the institutionalized centerpiece of social commerce. We are all compelled to "feel your pain." Others have recognized this phenomenon as the "Oprahfication" or "Feminization" or "Emasculation" of the culture.
>
> —Gerald L. Rowles, Ph.D.,
> "Prescription for America: An Epidemic of Alexithymia"

I have tried getting in touch with my feelings, but I get no answer.

—Charles Krauthammer,
The Washington Post, May 11, 1990

Never examine your feelings, they're no help at all.

—Patty Hearst

The world is a comedy to those that think, a tragedy to those that feel.

—Horace Walpole, *Letters* (1903–5)

Feiffer, Jules (1929–)

Pulitzer Prize–winning cartoonist, novelist, playwright, and chronicler of urban *neurosis*. "I lead a professional life the success of which is based on my being bitterly disappointed in everything," he once said. Feiffer's articulate and introspective characters include Passionella, his signature dancer in the black leotard whose enormous breasts earn her movie stardom, and a man who invents a Lonely Machine that makes small talk and gives encouragement. Feiffer's cartoons have been compiled in various books, including the best-selling *Sick, Sick, Sick* (1958).

> Back then [in the 1950s], comedy was still working in a tradition that came out of World War I. . . . Comedy was mired in insults and gags. It was Bob Hope and Bing Cosby, Burns and Allen, Ozzie and Harriet. There was no such thing as comedy about relationships, nothing about the newly urban and collegiate Americans. What I was interested in was using humor as a reflection of one's own confusion, ambivalence, and dilemma, dealing with sexual life as one knew it to be.
>
> —Jules Feiffer

Fisher, Carrie (1956–)

American actress, novelist, and screenwriter, daughter of Debbie Reynolds and Eddie Fisher, who achieved early stardom as Princess Leia in the Star Wars pictures. The drug addiction, manic depression, and matrimonial mishaps she has chronicled in a series of autobiographical novels beginning with the best-selling *Postcards from the Edge* (1987) have apparently not addled her quirky wit and highly cultivated sense of the absurd.

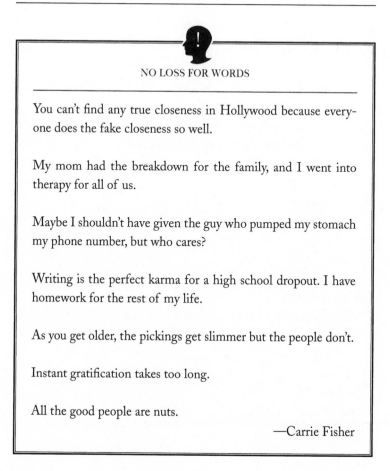

NO LOSS FOR WORDS

You can't find any true closeness in Hollywood because everyone does the fake closeness so well.

My mom had the breakdown for the family, and I went into therapy for all of us.

Maybe I shouldn't have given the guy who pumped my stomach my phone number, but who cares?

Writing is the perfect karma for a high school dropout. I have homework for the rest of my life.

As you get older, the pickings get slimmer but the people don't.

Instant gratification takes too long.

All the good people are nuts.

—Carrie Fisher

flasher
One who compulsively exposes his genitals to strangers.

It was so cold in Manhattan today, the flashers in Times Square were just describing themselves to people.

—David Letterman

See also *exhibitionist.*

flying saucers
Putative craft from outer space.

> It seems to me that the reports of flying saucers are far more
> likely to be attributable to the known, irrational characteristics
> of terrestrial intelligence, rather than to the unknown, rational
> characteristics of extra-terrestrial intelligence.
> —Richard Feynman, Cornell University lecture

food contact phobia
Common childhood aversion in which the slightest touching of
two different foods on the same plate causes disgust, gagging,
and occasional vomiting.

free association
Psychoanalytic technique for exploring the unconscious in
which the analysand says everything that comes to mind, no
matter how idiotic.

free-floating anxiety
Constant anxiety unrelated to a specific situation or danger.
See also *ambient fear.*

freek
Someone obsessed with getting things for free or at deep dis-
counts, e.g., compulsive coupon clippers, earlybird specialists,
perpetual contestants, "twofer" aficionados.

Freud, Sigmund (1856–1939)
Viennese neurologist whose theories that psychological problems are cause by unresolved childhood conflicts, and that
dreams provide clues to the nature of the psyche, became the basic of *psychoanalysis* and profoundly influenced modern thought,

particularly literature and literary criticism. Postmodern thought rejects most of his ideas and blames his jaundiced view of human nature for producing a "culture of shame." Dubbed "the Viennese Quack" by the writer Vladimir Nabokov half a century ago, Freud systematically distorted findings and fabricated case-histories. His psychoanalytic approach, which he described as "talking people into and out of things," has been largely supplanted by the use of brain-chemistry-altering medication, and his writings, if they are read at all, are now regarded as literature rather than science.

Freud was himself multiphobic and insanely superstitious: He believed in numerology and the occult, and was famously addicted to cocaine and tobacco. He placed himself behind the couch, out of the analysand's view, for two reasons: so as not to influence the patient's reactions, and because he hated being stared at.

> In America today, Freud's intellectual influence is greater than that of any other thinker. He presides over the mass media, the college classroom, the chatter at parties, the playgrounds of the middle classes where child rearing is a prominent and somewhat anxious topic of conversation.
>
> —Philip Rieff (1959)

> I reject completely the vulgar, shabby, fundamentally medieval world of Freud, with its crankish quest for sexual symbols (something like searching for Baconian acrostics in Shakespeare's work) and its bitter little embryos spying, from their natural nooks, upon the love life of their parents.
>
> —Vladimir Nabokov, *Speak, Memory* (1951)

> Freud is truly in a class of his own. Arguably no other notable figure in history was so fantastically wrong about nearly every

important thing he had to say. But, luckily for him, academics have been—and still are—infinitely creative in their efforts to whitewash his errors, even as lay readers grow increasingly dumbfounded by the entire mess.

—Todd Dufresne,
"Psychoanalysis Is Dead . . . So How Does That Make You Feel?"
Los Angeles Times, February 18, 2004

Our great detective of the unconscious was incompetent from the outset, no more astute, really, then Peter Sellers's bumbling Inspector Clouseau.

—Frederick Crews,
Unauthorized Freud: Doubters Confront a Legend (1998)

A man so dissatisfied with his own mother and father that he devoted his life to convincing everyone who would listen—or better still, talk—that their parents were just as bad.

—John Ralston Saul,
The Doubter's Companion (1994)

Freud was out of his fucking mind.

—Albert Ellis, *The New Yorker*, October 13, 2003

See also *Freudianism, Freudian slip, Oedipus Complex, psychoanalysis.*

Freudianism

Body of psychoanalytic doctrine propounded by *Sigmund Freud.*

Freudianism is much more nearly a religion than a science, inasmuch as the relation between analyst and patient has a great deal in common with that between priest and communicant at confessional, and such ideas as the Oedipus complex, the superego, the libido, and the id exert an effect upon the converted which is almost identical with what flows to the devout Christian from godhead, trinity, grace, and immortality.

—Robert Nisbet,
Prejudices: A Philosophical Dictionary (1982)

Freud's apostles begot apostates who in turn spawned heresies and a bemusing number of therapeutic sects, each claiming to have a piece of the true couch.

—R. Z. Sheppard, *Time* magazine, April 18, 1988

Freudianism is on the retreat because it isn't scientific and doesn't cure patients.

—Robert G. Salter

Freudian slip (aka "parapraxis")

According to *Freudianism,* a slip of the tongue that reveals repressed emotions. Many modern psychologists prefer a simpler explanation: under stress, we suffer neurological glitches—information processing errors—that make us utter a similar but inappropriate word.

When a member of my family complains to me of having bitten his tongue, pinched a finger, or the like, he does not get the sympathy he hopes for but instead the question "Why did you do that?"

—Sigmund Freud,
The Psychopathology of Everyday Life (1901)

I was having dinner with my mother last night, and I made a classic Freudian slip. I meant to say, "Would you please pass the salt?" But it came out, "You ruined my life!"

—Jonathan Katz

G

gallows humor
Something said or done to make light of tragedy. The human ability to joke about the most dire situations may be one of our most endearing qualities.
See also *humor.*

Garciaparra, Nomar (1973–)
All-star major league shortstop known as much for his *personal rituals* as for hitting and fielding. He listens to the same music on the way to the ballpark and takes the same route every day, he always gets dressed the same way (putting his shoes and socks on in a specific order), always wears the same underwear, and refuses to wash his cap during the season. When he exits the dugout to take the field, he hops up the steps sideways, making sure to touch each one. In the field, as the pitcher begins his windup, Nomar removes his glove, spits on his hand, then replaces the glove. "It's important to be comfortable out there, and having a ritual makes me comfortable," he explains. He claims that his routines, rather than being superstitious, actually eliminate superstition. "If I do everything the same every day, I can't blame a bad day at the plate on the fact that I didn't do the routine." (See *denial.*)

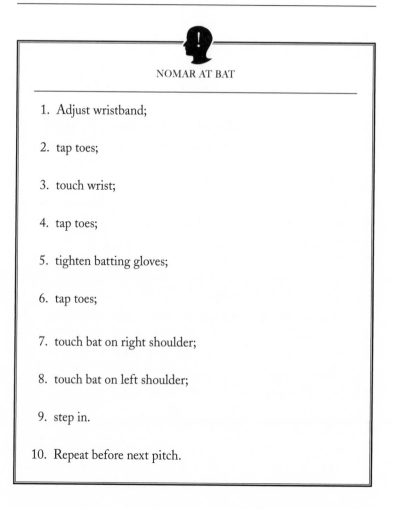

NOMAR AT BAT

1. Adjust wristband;

2. tap toes;

3. touch wrist;

4. tap toes;

5. tighten batting gloves;

6. tap toes;

7. touch bat on right shoulder;

8. touch bat on left shoulder;

9. step in.

10. Repeat before next pitch.

See also *obsessive-compulsive disorder, personal ritual, superstition.*

gay-bashing
See *homophobia.*

gaydar

Supposed intuitive ability of gay males to recognize one another—even if ostensibly straight—based on such indicators as a campy sense of humor or frequent references to "Mother."

> The earliest form of gaydar—that sissy sixth sense that tells you another of your breed is somewhere in the vicinity—was discovered by me, I am proud to say, in gym class in the late fifties. The last kid chosen for volleyball, or any other kind of ball except the one I wanted to be chosen for, was invariably me. The next-to-last kid, the one the other team got, was invariably the other gay kid in the class.
>
> —Bruce Vilanch

generalized anxiety disorder

Chronic anxiety with no specific cause combined with a vague sense of dread, often accompanied by irrational fears and increased heart rate and blood pressure. Sufferers tend to self-medicate.

See also *self-medication.*

Gigante, Vincent "the Chin" (1928–)

Legendary New York Mafia boss whose feigned mental illness kept him out of prison for over thirty years. In 1997, after a long series of competency hearings and other court appearances in which he performed his twitching, muttering, crazy act, the man who became famous for strolling the streets of New York in his bathrobe and pajamas was finally convicted of racketeering and sentenced to twelve years in prison.

Glover, Crispin (1964–)

Edgy, chalk-skinned American actor, writer, and director known for his portrayals of a tormented neurotic in *River's Edge* (1986), a nerdy father in *Back to the Future* (1985), and the title role in

Willard (2003). He is somewhat less known for his eccentric off-camera life, which includes an all-black wardrobe and a gynecological examination table in his living room.

> I can kick! I can kick!
>
> —Crispin Glover, karate-kicking inches
> from David Letterman's face on
> *Late Night with David Letterman,* July 28, 1987

gluttony
See *eating disorder.*

gonzo
Bizarre, idiosyncratic, over-the-top style, chiefly in participatory journalism. The term was coined by Bill Cardoso in 1971 and popularized by Hunter S. Thompson.

go postal
American slang for losing control and doing something violent.

> JERRY: Let me ask you something. What do you do for a living, Newman?
> NEWMAN: I'm a United States postal worker.
> JERRY: Aren't those the guys that always go crazy and come back with a gun and shoot everybody?
> NEWMAN: Sometimes . . .
> JERRY: Why is that?
> NEWMAN: Because the mail never stops. It just keeps coming and coming and coming, there's never a let-up. It's relentless. Every day it piles up more and more and more! And you gotta get it out but the more you get it out the more it keeps coming in. And then the bar code reader breaks and it's Publisher's Clearing House day!
> —*Seinfeld,* "The Old Man"

greeting card

Preprinted decorative card bearing a sentimental message or poem for a holiday or special occasion. In the United States, greeting cards are a major industry because of Americans' unwillingness or inability to put their own sentiments in their own words. They are sold in department stores, drugstores, and supermarkets under such categories as Troubled Love and Pet Bereavement. Surveys indicate that people actually send themselves Valentine cards to avoid embarrassment.

> Greeting cards: When you care enough to send the very best, but not enough to actually *write* something.
> —Howard Ogden, *Pensamentoes, Volume II* (2003)

> Greeting cards are becoming our epic poetry.
> —James B. Twitchell, *Carnival Culture: The Trashing of Taste in America* (1992)

> Sis, even if you were adopted, I'd still love you . . .
> —greeting card, American Greetings (1997)

groupie

Dedicated *fan*, usually a teenage girl, who follows a rock group or professional sports team hoping to have sex with one or some or all members, serially or simultaneously.
See also *celebriphilia*.

Grübeleien

German word for a not entirely unpleasant form of brooding; a sort of inward-directed *schadenfreude*, i.e., perverse delight in one's *own* troubles.

> I indulged in what Germans call *Grübeleien*, a word difficult to translate, connoting aimless broodings focused on oneself, with

the outside world serving only as a resonance box for unbridled egoism.

—Nicolas Slonimsky,

Perfect Pitch (1988)

guideline creep
Maddening tendency of experts to raise the bar on health-habit standards just when you thought you were doing okay, as when the U.S. government increased from a half hour to an hour the minimum amount of daily exercise necessary for optimum cardiovascular health.

guilt
Traditionally, remorse over having done something wrong; self-reproach for some moral failure. Modernly, a chronic, free-floating, unarticulated malaise, a festering sense of existential worthlessness. And then you feel guilty for feeling guilty.

> The child's physical functions—first those of defecation, then his sexual desires and activities—are weighed down by moral considerations. The child is made to feel guilty with regard to these functions, and since the sexual urge is present in every person from childhood on, it becomes a constant source of the feeling of guilt. What is the function of this feeling of guilt? It serves to break the child's will and to drive it into submission. The parents use it, although unintentionally, as a means to make the child submit. There is nothing more effective in breaking any person than to give him the conviction of wickedness. The more guilty one feels, the more easily one submits because the authority has proven its own power by its right to accuse. What appears as a feeling of guilt, then, is actually the fear of displeasing those of whom one is afraid. This feeling of guilt is the only one which most people experience as a moral problem, while the genuine moral problem, that of realizing one's

potentialities, is lost from sight. Guilt is reduced to disobedience and is not felt as that which it is in a genuine moral sense, self-mutilation.

—Erich Fromm,
"Individual and Social Origins of Neurosis" (1944)

Guilt is a growth market. It's developed by the diet industry, circulated by the health merchandisers, recycled by environmentalists. And in its improved version, targeted to the most reliable of consumers: mothers.

—Ellen Goodman,
The Boston Globe, October 11, 1990

I carry around such a load of nonspecific guilt that every time the metal detector beeps, I always have a wild fear that this trip I absentmindedly packed a Luger.

—Dan Greenburg, *How to Be a Jewish Mother* (1965)

I feel guilty about getting the pleasure [from a massage]. I feel like I don't deserve it so I talk. It stops me from enjoying it.

—George in *Seinfeld,* "The Note"

See also *Kafka, Franz; street guilt; survivor guilt.*

guilt sponge
One particularly susceptible to guilt, e.g., anyone raised Jewish or Catholic.

Gumping
Muddling through complacently in the hope that good luck or divine intervention will produce a favorable outcome. Named for Forrest Gump, the semiretarded title character of a 1994 feature film who managed to succeed through fantastic luck.

guru

Hindi for a spiritual teacher and guide; American slang for a charismatic mentor.

Gurus often tell us exactly what we want to hear. "There is no death." That is the primary message of spirituality gurus. Better yet, this relief from fear of death is easily obtained. The spiritual peace and enlightenment offered by pop gurus doesn't require a lifetime of discipline. It requires only that you suspend your critical judgment, attend their lectures and workshops and buy their books or tapes.

What's wrong with a phenomenon that brings comfort to so many people? That's a bit like asking what's wrong with a lobotomy, a steady diet of happy pills. The rise of charismatic authority figures is always disconcerting, especially when they malign rationalism and exhort us to abandon critical thinking in order to realize spiritual growth. Pop gurus prey on existential anxieties and thrive when our fear of being alone and mortal in an indifferent universe is stronger than our judgment. No one who seeks worship, however covertly, deserves respect. Argue with them, please.

—Wendy Kaminer, "Why We Love Gurus,"
Newsweek, October 20, 1997

Believe those who seek the truth, but doubt those who find it.

—André Gide

H

half-empty/half-full

The way you describe the proverbial glass of water is a gauge of your worldview.

People seem not to see that their opinion of the world is also a confession of character.

—Ralph Waldo Emerson, *The Conduct of Life* (1860)

See also *optimism/pessimism.*

happiness

Highly coveted but elusive state that resists precise definition because it varies over time, among individuals, and across cultures, though most people would agree that it is transitory. Its opposite, unhappiness, is much easier to define and seems to be a lot more prevalent. Historical note: In America, the notion that happiness is attainable got a big boost when the Declaration of Independence made its pursuit an "inalienable right."

Happiness is an imaginary condition, formerly often attributed by the living to the dead, now usually attributed by adults to children, and by children to adults.

—Thomas Szasz, *The Myth of Mental Illness* (1960)

Where was it ever promised us that life on this earth can ever be easy, free from conflict and uncertainty, devoid of anguish and wonder and pain? Those who seek the folly of unrelieved "happiness"—who fear moods, who shun solitude, who do not know the dignity of occasional depression—can find bliss easily enough: in tranquilizing pills, or in senility. The purpose of life is not to be happy.

—Leo Rosten

Happiness ain't a thing in itself—it's only a contrast with something that ain't pleasant. And so, as soon as the novelty is over and the force of the contrast dulled, it ain't happiness any longer, and you have to get something fresh.

—Mark Twain

Happiness isn't something you experience, it's something you remember.

—Oscar Levant

Happiness is for idiots.

—Charles de Gaulle

It takes a lot of guts to be happy.

—Nadja Salerno-Sonnenberg, "Speaking in Strings"

happy violence
Term coined by George Gerbner of the Annenberg School for Communication at the University of Pennsylvania to describe violence in an otherwise benign context, as in children's cartoons.

Children's cartoons are full of mayhem—thirty-two acts per hour. Cartoon humor appears to be the sugar coating on the pill of cool and happy violence.

—George Gerbner

See also *information sickness, mean world syndrome, television.*

Harold
One with a morbid interest (as it were) in death, cemeteries, and the grief of total strangers. *Harolds* are named for the death-obsessed character played by Bud Cort in Hal Ashby's 1971 cult film *Harold and Maude.* Harolds make a hobby of "Harolding," i.e., showing up uninvited at funerals, wakes, and memorial services.

hathos
Pleasurable hatred of someone or something, especially of annoying celebrities or powerful organizations.
See also *schadenfreude.*

heightened illness concern
See *hypochondria, worried well.*

hedonistic treadmill
Habituating effect of increasing wealth. According to Princeton economist Alan Krueger, you're quick to adapt to improved economic circumstances, the novelty of new possessions wears off quickly, and losing them makes you more unhappy than getting them made you happy.

> Every increased possession loads us with new weariness.
> —John Ruskin

> If life is a car traveling down the road at 55 mph, money and fame will change the color of the car, but it won't change its speed or direction. It is interesting to note that most entertainment whiz kids buy and sell their red Ferraris within a year; they quickly convert to gray Audis and Lexuses and stay with their brands thereafter.
> —Douglas Coupland, *The New Republic,* December 12, 1994

See also *affluenza.*

heterophobia
Fear or hatred of heterosexuality.

> Women's bodies are possessed by men. Women are forced into involuntary childbearing because men, not women, control women's reproductive functions. Women are an enslaved population—the crop we harvest is children, the fields we work are houses. Women are forced into committing sexual acts with men that violate integrity because the universal religion—

contempt for women—has as its first commandment that
women exist purely as sexual fodder for men.
    —Andrea Dworkin, "Pornography: The New Terrorism" (1978)

See also *homophobia.*

high-maintenance
Difficult to get along with; demanding; needy.

> You told him I was high maintenance? Why did you do that? It
> took me seven years to get my life together.
>   —Richard Lewis to *Larry David* on *Curb Your Enthusiasm*

Hitchcock, Alfred (1899–1980)
One of the greatest directors in the history of the cinema, the
"master of suspense" who directed fifty-three features over half a
century, and a seething mass of fetishes and phobias: hypochondriac, acrophobic, claustrophobic, agoraphobic, morbidly obese
all his life, he feared insanity, he feared surprises, he feared being
a bore, and he feared seeming pretentious (the reason he never
used a viewfinder). He was fanatically secretive, he detested
small children, he had a horror of vomiting, and he would gag at
the smell of a boiled egg. And, of course, he was obsessed with
murder.

He was the youngest son of a prosperous London greengro-
cer. A Cockney and a Catholic, he received a strict religious up-
bringing and was sent to St. Ignatius College, a Jesuit secondary
school. Hitchcock often reminisced about punishment at the
hands of the priests. "One was beaten with a cane made of
gutta-percha, which was similar to hard rubber. The sting was
absolute. I can feel it now."

A schoolmate described Alfred as "a lonely fat boy who
smiled and looked at you as if he could see straight through

you." An observer rather than a participant, he watched games from the sidelines without joining in. He developed an elaborate inner life instead. He read voraciously: Dickens, Poe, H. G. Wells, Conan Doyle, Shaw, and G. K. Chesterton, whose Father Brown mysteries probably sharpened his fascination for criminal behavior. He was also captivated by the fledging "motion pictures" and read all the film journals he could find.

After training as an engineer, Hitchcock worked at an electrical cable company and attended art classes at night. He took his portfolio to the London branch of an American film company, Famous Players-Lasky, and was hired as a title-card designer. In 1925, he directed his first feature, *The Pleasure Garden,* and he made the first British talkie, *Blackmail,* in 1929.

During the 1930s a rapid succession of British films brought him international acclaim: *The Man Who Knew Too Much* (1934), *The 39 Steps* (1935), *Sabotage* (1936), *Secret Agent* (1936), and *The Lady Vanishes* (1938). David O. Selznick brought Hitchcock to Hollywood in 1938, and together they made *Rebecca* (1940), *Spellbound* (1945), and *The Paradine Case* (1947). It was a fruitful collaboration: All three pictures were successful, and *Rebecca* won the Best Picture Oscar, but they never became friends. "He seems a nice person," Selznick wrote, "but he is hardly the kind of man you would want along on a camping trip."

By the time shooting began Hitchcock had already mapped out every camera angle and cut. He was always in complete control on the set, relaxed but reserved, rarely displaying a temper. He claimed to be "incapable" of showing anger, and avoided any sort of confrontation, preferring to deal with people through intermediaries whenever possible. One day an assistant director on *Lifeboat* (1944) informed him that the women on the set were complaining that Tallulah Bankhead was climbing in and out of the boat wearing no underpants. Hitchcock refused to intervene, fearing an argument with the volatile actress.

"It isn't my department," he said.

"Well then, whose department is it?" asked the assistant.

"It's either Hairdressing or Makeup," Hitchcock replied.

The only truly famous director of his era, Hitchcock's name above the title of a film could guarantee box office success, in part because the master of suspense was also a master of *self-promotion*. He cultivated a droll, avuncular persona through brief "signature" cameos, beginning with *The Lodger* in 1926. Audiences so anticipated these appearances that he showed up early in the picture so as not, as he put it, "to hold them in suspense for the wrong reason." He'd be on the screen for a few seconds, walking a dog, boarding a bus, carrying a cello. *Lifeboat* presented a problem in this regard, because the entire picture is set in a small boat adrift at sea. Hitchcock's first idea was to have himself drifting by as a dead body, but he feared he might not be able to float. His solution was to put photos of himself in a newspaper found on the boat as the "before" and "after" models in an ad for a fictitious diet drug.

He became even more familiar from his trademark self-caricature, the line-silhouette he magically stepped into at the start of each episode of *Alfred Hitchcock Presents,* his popular television series which aired from 1955 to 1962 (and is still in syndication). His wry framing monologues further endeared him to the American public, as did his mock disdain for the "spohnsah."

Our play tonight is a blend of mystery and medicine. It follows this one-minute anesthetic . . .

Of course, just as no rose is complete without thorns, no show is complete without the following . . .

Tonight's story is about a man named Perry and follows after a minute called *tedious* . . .

Hitchcock was a lifelong practical joker. As a boy he'd pinned firecrackers to a schoolmate's trousers; as an adult he pretended to nod off in public to test people's reactions—he once took Carole Lombard and Loretta Young to Chasen's and "fell asleep" during dinner. In his office he kept a latex replica of his own head which he would pull out to startle visitors.

Some of the jokes were sadistic. During the filming of *The 39 Steps,* he handcuffed Robert Donat and Madeleine Carroll together and pretended to lose the key. And he once bet a prop man that he wouldn't be able to spend a night alone in the studio. Hitchcock handcuffed him to a camera and produced a bottle of brandy "to see him through the night." The next morning the man was found weeping, his clothing befouled. Hitchcock had put laxative in the brandy. A friend later tried the same trick on Hitchcock, giving him a bottle of laxative-spiked brandy as a gift. When Hitchcock failed to mention it after several days, the friend asked if he'd tried the brandy. "Oh yes, I'd almost forgot," Hitchcock replied. "My mother is ill, and when the doctor prescribed brandy, we gave her yours."

Hitchcock often recounted a childhood incident: When he was five or six, in punishment for some minor offense, his father sent him to the police station with a note. The officer read it and placed him in a cell for five minutes, telling him, "This is what we do to naughty little boys." Hitchcock said he never forgot the sound of the heavy cell door clanging shut behind him, and he often cited this trauma as the root of his lifelong fear of authority, and as the source of a recurring theme in his films: the innocent man unjustly arrested and imprisoned. Hitchcock portrays authority figures as petty and corrupt: His lawyers, judges, politicians, and policemen come off little better than his murderers and spies.

He was compulsively neat, a self-described "ashtray emptier" who washed his hands frequently, always using two or three towels to dry them and to wipe the basin and faucets. When, after an audience with the pope, his wife came down with strep throat, Hitchcock ascribed it to her having kissed the pope's ring because, after all, you never knew where it might have been.

He had few friends. His pleasures were simple and solitary. He often attended the theater alone. He was an avid reader who usually found himself in bed with a book by nine o'clock. And he was a secret eater who could polish off three steaks and a quart of ice cream in one sitting. But no eggs. "I'm frightened of eggs," he once said, "worse than frightened, they revolt me. That white round thing without any holes . . . have you ever seen anything more revolting than an egg yolk breaking and spilling its yellow liquid? Blood is jolly, red. But egg yolk is yellow, revolting. I've never tasted it."

Hitchcock seemed to have little sense of his own greatness: The interval between the completion of a film and its release was always torture. He worried that if the film flopped, he would never be allowed to make another. He was once so anxious about an upcoming speech to university students that he arranged in advance to have a telephone call interrupt him early in the talk, but once he got going he warmed to the task and wound up staying for several hours.

Hitchcock named Flaubert's repressed bourgeois housewife Emma Bovary as his favorite fictional character, and he seemed to follow Flaubert's advice to writers to "be regular and orderly like a bourgeois, so that you may be violent and original in your work." In contrast to his violent and original films, Hitchcock's domestic life was indeed regular and orderly: By most accounts he was a devoted husband and an attentive if not affectionate father. He had been a virgin when he married film editor Alma Reville when they were both twenty-five, and it seems he was never unfaithful, though he had crushes on a succession of leading ladies, and once boasted that Ingrid Bergman had pleaded in vain for his attentions. Though he was a rich man—he invested his movie money wisely and became a major stockholder in Universal upon the sale of *Alfred Hitchcock Presents*—he lived quietly, at least by Hollywood standards: He owned a relatively modest house in Bel Air, and aside from an extensive wine cellar, he had no extravagances.

At the end of his life he began drinking heavily, perhaps to medicate the dual torments of arthritis and senility. He told and retold the same anecdotes, his voice a weak monotone, his deadpan hardened into a frozen gaze. He died in 1980 at the age of eighty.

François Truffaut, whose book-length interview of Hitchcock first appeared in 1962 and remains a rich source of information about the otherwise reticent director, saw him as a "deeply vulnerable, sensitive and emotional man." Is that the key? Did Hitchcock impose his vulnerabilities on us, or just evoke our own? Was he an impish purveyor of the macabre who took sadistic pleasure in torturing audiences on the rack of suspense? (He once admitted that he enjoyed playing moviegoers "like a great organ," and that he thought of them as "moron masses.") Was his genius born of mighty demons, or was it all just technique? Did he merely want to make us squirm, or was he confronting us with profound existential questions?

Critics and cineastes will doubtless continue the debate, but if, as Truffaut remarked, Hitchcock's films had "inner fire and cool surfaces," so did their author: When asked if he was ever afraid, Hitchcock would reply, "Always."

> Hitchcock . . . was a singular man—in his spirit, his morality,
> and his obsessions. Unlike Chaplin, Ford, Rossellini, or Hawks,
> he was a neurotic, and it could not have been easy for him to
> impose his neuroses on the whole world.
>
> —François Truffaut

I've become a body of films, not a man. I am all those films.
—Alfred Hitchcock

hissy fit
Southern colloquialism for temper tantrum. Want to feminize a man? Describe him not as "getting angry" or "flipping out," but as "throwing a *hissy fit*."
See also *adult temper tantrum*.

holiday newsletter
Gratuitous annual report of family doings.

"Lucinda turned nineteen this year and took fearless charge of her direction and priorities . . ."
I love holiday newsletters, and for all the wrong reasons, I admit it. My favorites are the pretentious ones. There's something cathartic about wallowing in other people's egomania, and it's fun to read between the lines. For instance I'd be willing to be that Lucinda (not her real name) took fearless charge of her direction and priorities by piercing several body parts.
—Diane White, *The Boston Globe*, December 29, 1996

hollow-tooth syndrome
Compulsion to torture oneself mentally, based on the fact that nothing fixes a thing so intensely in the memory as the wish to forget it. The masochistic urge to revisit past embarrassment, sometimes called *mnemophobia*, causes some sufferers to actually cry out the instant the memory occurs.

homophobia
Fear or hatred of homosexuality. Some psychologists believe that rabid homophobes are unsure of their own sexuality.

Most gay bashers will be wearing what gay people had on four years earlier—only in Polyester with a Penney's label.

—Paul Rudnick

See also *heterophobia*.

hope
A wish accompanied by expectation of its fulfillment.

Hope is the feeling you have that the feeling you have isn't permanent.

—Jean Kerr, *Finishing Touches* (1974)

False hope is better than no hope.

—Howard Ogden, *Pensamentoes, Volume II* (2003)

hopelessness
Overwhelming feeling of futility and despair.

Isn't it the moment of most profound doubt that gives birth to new certainties? Perhaps hopelessness is the very soil that nourishes human hope; perhaps one could never find sense in life without first experiencing its absurdity.

—Václav Havel, "Anatomy of a Reticence"

See also *depression, doubt*.

hostility
Animosity, often self-defeating.

A small case of mood poisoning. Must be something I hate.

—Bruce Wagner, *Wild Palms*, May 17, 1993

hubris

Overweening pride; *self-destructive* arrogance. In Greek tragedy, insolence toward the gods that brings divine retribution.

huffing

Practice of inhaling fumes from readily available household products such as glue, solvent, nail polish, or air freshener, popular among young adolescents dying for a *buzz*. According to a study by the American Academy of Pediatrics, on average children are twelve years old when they first hear about huffing, and about one in four of those surveyed said their friends huff. Huffing can cause severe brain damage and can lead to further substance abuse.

Hughes, Howard (Howard Robard Hughes Jr., 1905–1976)

American industrialist, aviator, and movie producer who degenerated from fascinating eccentric to grotesque recluse.

After a difficult birth, his mother was advised not to have any more children, and she was thus overprotective of her only child, instilling many of his lifelong phobias: She actually took "Sonny" out of town during epidemics, and he learned to pretend to be sick to stop his parents' arguments. He was sent to the best private schools, but was an indifferent student with few friends. Quiet and withdrawn, he spent most of his time alone, tinkering with mechanical things (his father provided him with his own workbench at the Hughes Tool Company plant, where he also learned how to operate a lathe). The family fortune derived from a drill that revolutionized oil exploration and eventually earned hundreds of millions of dollars.

Hughes's mother died in 1922, at the age of thirty-nine, of complications from minor surgery, and his father died less than two years later of a heart attack at age fifty-four. The early deaths of his parents further contributed to his *hypochondria* and convinced Hughes that he was destined for a similar fate. At any rate, he was suddenly an eighteen-year-old multimillionaire, answerable to no one. He assumed control of the Hughes Tool Company and bought out his relatives, an act that caused an irreparable estrangement. He married Houston debutante Ella Rice in 1925, but she divorced him three years later.

Hughes had a lifelong passion for aviation. Shy and jittery on the ground, he was relaxed and assured in a cockpit. He took a $250-a-month job as a copilot for American Airways under an assumed name, but was forced to resign after only one flight when his true identity was revealed. In 1932 he got a job with American Airways as a baggage handler and pilot in training to find out how to run an airline (some say to escape the pressures of his life).

He was an aviation daredevil who won prizes and set records, including the around-the-world record in 1938 (three days, nineteen hours). When he heard that Charles Lindbergh had pilot's license number 69, he got the Commerce Department to lower the number of his own license from 4223 to 80. He suffered five serious crashes, one of which, in July 1946, caused injuries that he wasn't expected to survive. He was given morphine and codeine for the pain, beginning a serious narcotics addiction. He attributed his eventual recovery to drinking large quantities of fresh orange juice, consumed immediately after squeezing (he refused the orange juice in the hospital because he couldn't be sure it was fresh, and insisted that oranges be sliced and squeezed in his room).

After the 1946 crash he grew increasingly secretive and reclusive. His last public appearance was in 1947, for the first and only flight of the *Spruce Goose,* the nickname of the Hercules flying boat, the largest plane ever built. Actually made of birch plywood, the 180-ton plane, designed to carry two battalions of soldiers nonstop from Honolulu to Tokyo, was a colossal flop: Hughes lost $7.5 million on its development and spent an additional $1 million a year to mothball it.

Hughes began producing films at the age of nineteen with no experience but lots of capital (Ben Hecht dubbed him "the sucker with the money"). He also had an eye for talent (he "discovered" Jean Harlow) and definite ideas on how to make a movie.

Hell's Angels (1930) would be the first epic of the sound era, and Hughes was determined to make it his way, no matter what the cost. He shot and reshot scenes until he got what he wanted, though much of the time he didn't *know* what he wanted. He hired his own private air force, with dozens of pilots (three of whom were killed in the course of filming) and a hundred mechanics to keep 'em flying. At one point he moved the entire production to northern California because he wanted white, puffy clouds as the backdrop for an aerial combat scene. All told it cost almost $4 million (of Hughes Tool Company profits), by far the highest movie budget to date. By one estimate he shot over two million feet of film for a fifteen-thousand-foot feature. Though it didn't come near recouping its cost, *Hell's Angels* was a box office smash and earned Hughes the grudging respect of the Hollywood that had scorned him. Hughes also produced *The Front Page* (1931), *Scarface* (1932), and *The Outlaw* (1941), for which he built interest by designing a special bra for star Jane Russell and by delaying release while battling censors, thereby turning a mediocre movie into a box office hit. As a filmmaker he had the unique luxury of time: He spent six years personally editing *Jet Pilot* starring John Wayne and Janet Leigh so that when the film was finally released in 1957 most of the aerial sequences had been cut because of aviation advances in the interim.

As a businessman Hughes was more autocrat than manager. He wrote or dictated thousands of memoranda establishing elaborate rules and procedures for everything: how to file documents, the proper form for various written communications, the maintenance of lists ("reminder list," "master reminder list," "special reminder list"), the processing of incoming telephone calls, etc. He also devised a classification system to keep his business dealings private ("Secret," "Confidential," "Restricted").

He gave code names to his close associates (Jean Peters was "Major Bertrandez") and demanded they register in "locate books" the telephone numbers where they could be reached at all times. He once had a private line installed in the home of one executive so he wouldn't have to compete with the teenagers in the house. Though he paid generous salaries and fringe benefits, he had little regard for other people and believed that every man has his price. Robert Maheu, a longtime aide, quoted Hughes as saying, "I, Howard Hughes, can buy any man in the world, or I can destroy him." But Hughes rarely if ever personally fired anyone.

The Hughes Tool Company was the crown jewel of his empire, providing the cash to finance his other interests. Contrary to his carefully contrived image of a shrewd businessman, all his other companies lost money—except Hughes Aircraft, which he ignored—and over the years he was swindled out of millions of dollars by employees. (At their height the various Hughes enterprises employed over fifty thousand people.) He bought Trans World Airlines and nearly bankrupted the then third largest airline in the world (he would often cancel a scheduled flight and commandeer the plane for his own use). In 1967 he spent $20 million for gold and silver mining properties in California and Nevada, almost all of which proved worthless.

One of the few things in life Hughes seemed to enjoy was the process of deal-making. His main strategy was to wear opponents down by dragging out negotiations. When he contracted for a new airplane for TWA he wanted to call it the Golden Arrow, but it was named the Convair 880 instead—in commemoration of the number of bargaining sessions with Hughes it took to close the deal, joked a company executive.

The bottom line on Hughes as a businessman: he probably lost a billion dollars on failed ventures, though to this day his reputation remains that of a brilliant entrepreneur. He cultivated the image of a rugged individualist, but in fact he relied on special treatment from state and federal governments. Though he was admired for not resting on his inheritance, if he had just invested it conservatively his estate would have been worth billions rather than the estimated $600 million to $900 million.

Hughes liked to do things that were guaranteed to get attention, yet he shunned personal publicity; he knew how to create intense public curiosity, but he abhorred scrutiny. He was acutely aware of his image and once reprimanded his PR man after seeing himself referred to in a magazine as a "millionaire" rather than a "billionaire." But when *Life* magazine profiled him, he bought up all 175,000 copies and had them burned, and when an independent producer made a documentary about him, Hughes bought the film before it could be aired.

Hughes never had a long-term *relationship*. He employed an "entertainment staff" to procure young women, who were required to sign a release before Hughes would meet them. He had them followed by private detectives who submitted detailed reports of their activities, and when one became ill, he would insist that she see his doctor so he could obtain a report on her condition. He was partial to starlets and actresses, including Billie Dove, Marian Marsh, Terry Moore (who claims Hughes married her aboard a yacht at sea), Ida Lupino, Lillian Bond, Mary Rogers, Carole Lombard, Ava Gardner, Ginger Rogers, Katharine Hepburn (he landed his plane on a Bel Air Country Club fairway to impress her), Gene Tierney, and Jean Peters, whom he married in 1958 to avoid being declared incompetent by his longtime aide Noah Dietrich (under California law, an involuntary commitment would have been impossible without the consent of Hughes's wife). They lived apart for most of their thirteen-year marriage. She could not call him directly and had to make an appointment to see him. Their divorce settlement gave her between $70,000 and $140,000 a year for twenty years, the actual amount depending on the annual cost of living index. She remarried two months after their divorce became final in 1971.

Hughes was riddled with obsessions, *phobias,* and *delusions.* He was pathologically indecisive: He could take an hour to decide what to order from a menu, and he agonized endlessly over major decisions, often delaying so long that the matter would become moot. He was a world-class microphobe who eliminated as much human contact as possible. Not only did he refuse to touch doorknobs, he imagined he could create a "germ-free zone" for himself by means of what he called "insulation," layers of Kleenex and paper towels covering anything he touched. To prevent what he called the "backflow" of germs, he mandated procedures for handling everything he came in contact with. Whenever an attendant handed him something, it had to be wrapped in what Hughes called a "paddle," a layer of Kleenex. He issued a three-page memo describing the proper technique for opening a can, down to the preparation of the table, the scrubbing of the can, and specific "fallout rules," i.e., the correct positioning of the body while handling the can to prevent contamination. Another memo described the sterile method of buying groceries (a three-man operation), and once, when he pronounced a grilled cheese sandwich the best he'd ever tasted, aides were obliged to issue a report (titled "Grilled Cheese Sandwiches") describing precisely how it had been made, including the fact that the cook was admonished by Hughes aides to make sure the knife and cutting board used to make the sandwich were free from the odor of onion.

Fearing eavesdroppers, Hughes conducted meetings in cars late at night on deserted streets, or in rest rooms where he could run water to defeat any hidden microphones. He imagined that the only safe telephones in New York were at the Waldorf-

Astoria, and once, before he would discuss an important transaction with an employee, Hughes ordered him to check into a room where he would be "completely private," which meant with empty rooms on either side.

Hughes told his employees what to eat and where to park their cars. He promulgated elaborate driving rules for his motor pool: Passengers were to be escorted to and from the vehicle and seated in the back, except in cases of car sickness. The speed was never to exceed thirty-five miles per hour, and was to be drastically reduced "when crossing any bump, dip, swale, ditch, railroad track or any uneven part of any road." If the passenger was a woman, the speed on rough roads was to be reduced even further, because Hughes believed that jarring motions damaged the breasts. If a member of an employee's family had a contagious disease, the employee was barred from the office until the family member recovered.

No, Howard Hughes was not a *people person*. At the 1972 telephone press conference convened to debunk Clifford Irving's hoax autobiography, reporters quizzed Hughes on a variety of subjects. In response to questions about aviation he recalled minute details, but when asked about former close associates, he couldn't remember a single one. His contributions to charity were minuscule as a percentage of his great wealth. In 1953 he set up the Hughes Medical Institute, ostensibly to study major diseases, but actually to avoid income taxes.

After Hughes moved to Las Vegas in 1966, he got in the habit of watching late-night movies on television. But the local station went off the air every night at 1:00 a.m., and Hughes wanted to watch around the clock. So, after unsuccessful pleas to the station to "stay open" later, he bought it (for $3.6 million) and immediately expanded its movie policy. He likewise bought the Desert Inn when the management asked him to vacate the block of rooms that housed him and his staff. At one point he somehow got the idea that children at the annual Desert Inn Easter egg hunt were going to riot and destroy the hotel and casino, and offered to donate $50,000 to move the event.

In his final years he lived in almost total isolation, conducting business exclusively by memorandum or telephone so that nobody really knew if he was dead or alive. He ordered all windows and unused doors sealed to eliminate dust, and had thick drapes installed to block out sunlight.

His substance abuse got worse. He stored his drugs and syringes in a metal box within easy reach of his bed, which he left only to go to the toilet. He dissolved codeine tablets in water and self-injected the solution, and popped handfuls of ten-milligram Valium tablets, which he called "blue bombers." His use of codeine caused severe constipation and he sometimes sat on the toilet so long he fell asleep.

His health deteriorated drastically. He suffered from severe dehydration and malnutrition. His personal hygiene was nonexistent: he had long toenails and fingernails, rotting teeth, gums oozing pus. He was covered with bedsores, bruises, and countless needle tracks from intravenous codeine shots, though he ultimately lacked the strength to inject himself. Postmortem X rays revealed broken hypodermic needles embedded in both arms. There was an open sore on his scalp where a tumor had been knocked off. He weighed ninety-three pounds and his body had shrunk several inches from its original six feet, four inches. "Kidney failure" was the official cause of death, but it could have been any number of things.

Ironically, his wealth and power had kept him a prisoner of his own fixations. If there had been someone who cared about him, he or she might have intervened, but he had no friends and was estranged from his family. Those around him used his fantasies and delusions to control him. He died alone, regressed to infancy, the demented product of his own obsessions. Only twenty-five people attended his funeral.

He'd been obsessed with his will for most of his adult life. He destroyed two valid wills executed as a young man, and as he grew older, though he wrote and rewrote new wills many times, he signed none of them, precipitating one of the longest, most expensive, and most chaotic probate fights in history, with over a thousand claimants, including twenty-two cousins and half a dozen putative offspring. Dozens of alleged wills were submitted, including Melvin Dummar's famous "Mormon Will," but none was probated, and it was finally ruled that Hughes died intestate. Thus, in yet another irony, most of his fortune went to the Hughes Medical Institute in Houston, the sham charity he had created as a tax dodge.

> Howard Hughes was able to afford the luxury of madness, like a man who not only thinks he is Napoleon, but hires an army to prove it.
> —Ted Morgan, *The New York Times Book Review*

> [Howard] Hughes . . . started as a very presentable young playboy with the world at his disposal, and ended as a starving, paranoid recluse trapped in a room watching old movies. Nor is this uncommon among the very rich: wealthy, paranoid, depressed recluses are a dime a dozen—Hughes was simply more theatrical about it, a result, perhaps, of his years in Hollywood.
> —Philip Slater, *Wealth Addiction* (1980)

human comedy, the
The broad sweep of human behavior. From *La Comédie Humaine* (1842), the title of a multivolume edition of the novels and short stories of Honoré de Balzac (1799–1850), who titled it as a contrary allusion to Dante's *Divine Comedy* (1321).

human condition, the
The real cause of most of our psychological problems, according to the nonpsychiatric view.

The state of man is changeableness, ennui, anxiety.

—Blaise Pascal

Nietzsche . . . thought that to live keenly we need to grasp life's tragic fragility and even its futility. Nietzsche's image for tragic man or woman was of one who keeps building sand castles even while aware of the incoming tide.

—Judith Shulevitz,
The New York Times Book Review,
February 10, 2002

He who despairs over an event is a coward, but he who holds hope for the human condition is a fool.

—Albert Camus

He who has never envied the vegetable has missed the human drama.

—E. M. Cioran

The psychiatrist Peter Kramer published a book called *Listening to Prozac,* which claimed that our understanding of neurochemistry was so advanced that we would soon be able to design— and no doubt to vary—our personalities according to our tastes. Henceforth there would be no more angst. He based his prediction upon the case histories of people given the supposed wonder drug who not merely recovered from depression but emerged with new, improved personalities.

Yet the prescription of the drug (and others like it) to millions of people has not noticeably reduced the sum total of human misery or the perplexity of life. A golden age of felicity has not arrived: and the promise of a pill for every ill remains, as it always will, unfulfilled. Anyone who had read his Shakespeare would not have been surprised by this disappointment. When Macbeth asks a physician:

Canst thou not minister to a
  mind diseased,
Pluck from the memory a
  rooted sorrow,
Raze out the written troubles
  of the brain,
And with some sweet
  oblivious antidote
Cleanse the stuffed bosom
  of that perilous stuff
Which weighs upon the heart?

The physician replies laconically, "Therein the patient / Must
minister to himself."

Every day, several patients ask me Macbeth's question with
regard to themselves—in less elevated language, to be sure—and
they expect a positive answer, but four centuries before neurochemistry was even thought of, and before any of the touted advances in neurosciences that allegedly gave us a new and better
understanding of ourselves, Shakespeare knew something that
we are increasingly loath to acknowledge: There is no technical
fix for the problems of humanity.

Those problems, he knew, are ineradicably rooted in our nature; and he atomized that nature with a characteristic genius
never since equaled: which is why every time we moderns con-
sult his works, we come away with a deeper insight into the
heart of our own mystery.

—Theodore Dalrymple, "Why Shakespeare Is for All Time"

No one, ever, can give the exact measure of his needs, his appre-
hensions, or his sorrows; and human speech is like a cracked
cauldron on which we bang out tunes that make bears dance,
when we want to move the stars to pity.

—Gustave Flaubert

Everything has been figured out, except how to live.

—Jean-Paul Sartre

Poop happens.

—Laura Schlessinger

It's a losin' fight.

—Chester A. Riley (William Bendix) in *The Life of Riley*

What can we take on trust in this uncertain life? Happiness, greatness, pride—nothing is secure, nothing keeps.

—Euripides, *Hecuba*

You fall out of your mother's womb, you crawl across open country under fire, and drop into your grave.

—Quentin Crisp

Maybe all one can do is hope to end up with the right regrets.

—Arthur Miller

See also *absurd, abyss, dark night of the soul, undertoad.*

human race, the
Those irrepressible primates, *homo sapiens.*

Man is a rope stretched between the animal and the Super-man—a rope over an abyss.

—Friedrich Nietzsche, *Thus Spake Zarathustra* (1891)

We are still monkeys.

—Freeman Dyson

All humans are out of their fucking minds—every single one of them.

—Albert Ellis, *The New Yorker,* October 13, 2003

humor

The quality that makes something funny; that which induces amusement by appealing to the sense of *the Absurd*. It's a commonplace that any attempt to analyze or even define humor kills it, but what the hell:

Humor is emotional chaos remembered in tranquility.
—James Thurber

Humor is not merely the telling of funny stories. It recognizes the vast difference between life as we imagine it and life as we live it, and between the fanciful and imposing impressions we have of ourselves and what we actually are.
—Brooks Atkinson, *Once Around the Sun* (1951)

Humor is, by its nature, more truthful than factual.
—P. J. O'Rourke

The truth I do not dare to know I muffle with a jest.
—Emily Dickinson

Humor is the best safety valve modern man has evolved; the more civilization, the more repression, the more need there is for humor.
—Sigmund Freud

Humor is just another defense against the universe.
—Mel Brooks

Outsiders develop humor as a defense. Why do you think most comedians are gay or Jewish?
—Paul Lynde

See also *gallows humor, Sullivan Syndrome.*

hurried-child syndrome
The neurotic result of parents pushing their children to excel academically while overscheduling their free time with countless extracurricular activities, i.e., hurrying them into adulthood.

hypergraphia
Uncontrollable urge to write, often exhibited by people with temporal lobe epilepsy. Unfortunately, the compulsion is rarely accompanied by talent.
See also *writer's block.*

hypochondria
Persistent, neurotic conviction that one is or is about to become ill, often involving experience of actual pain, though illness is neither present nor likely. The hypochondriac's conviction that he is sick persists despite the reassurances of a physician. Hypochondriacs tend toward selective perception, seeking out information that confirms their self-diagnosis and ignoring information that refutes it. When a hypochondriac receives test results indicating the absence of disease, he immediately suspects it to be a "false negative" and will change doctors rather than accept a clean bill of health. But hypochondriacs aren't malingerers—they sincerely believe they are ill, and their physical symptoms are often real, albeit without physiological cause.

Hypochondria is an expensive problem: *Studies* estimate that 60 to 90 percent of doctor visits are the result of self-limiting, stress-related symptoms—health problems that can't be effectively diagnosed or treated by conventional medicine.

> Studies show that at least a quarter of all patients report symptoms that appear to have no physical basis, and that one in ten continues to believe that he has a terminal disease even after the doctor has found him to be healthy. Experts say that between 3

and 6 percent of patients seen by primary-care physicians suffer from hypochondria, the irrational fear of illness. The number is likely growing, thanks to increased medical reporting in the media, which devotes particular attention to scary new diseases like SARS, and to the Internet, which provides a wealth of clinical information (and misinformation) that can help turn a concerned patient into a neurotic one. Nevertheless, hypochondria is rarely discussed in the doctor's office. The "worried well," as sufferers are sometimes called, typically feel insulted by any suggestion that their symptoms have a psychological basis. Most patients are given a formal diagnosis of hypochondria only after ten or so years of seeing physicians, if they get such a diagnosis at all. . . .

Many doctors and nurses make fun of hypochondriacs, calling them "crocks" and "turkeys." The favored epithet among interns and residents is "gomer," which stands for Get Out of My Emergency Room. Many doctors are relieved when a hypochondriac leaves them for another physician.

—Gerome Groopman, "Sick with Worry,"
The New Yorker, August 11, 2003

For each illness that doctors cure with medicine, they provoke ten in healthy people by inoculating them with the virus that is a thousand times more powerful than any microbe: the idea that one is ill.

—Marcel Proust, *In Search of Lost Time*
(1913–27; seven volumes)

Man has to suffer. When he has no real afflictions, he invents some.

—José Marti, *Adulterous Thoughts* (1883)

Many peptic ulcers and psychosomatic ailments are poems struggling to be born.

—Jack Leedy, psychologist

The best cure for hypochondria is to forget about your own body and get interested in someone else's.

—Goodman Ace

See also *heightened illness concern, Munchausen syndrome, worried well.*

I

id
According to Freud, the primitive, instinctive element of the psyche.
See also *ego, superego.*

identity crisis
Anxiety-producing conflict, usually in *adolescents,* over appropriate roles and expectations.

Who am I? How did I come into the world? Why was I not consulted?

—Søren Kierkegaard,
"Repetition: An Essay in Experimental Psychology"

I Knew It! syndrome
Compulsive repetition of a dumb mistake, named for Rupert Ritzik (Joe E. Ross) on *The Phil Silvers Show* (aka *Sergeant Bilko*) who, after falling for yet another of Bilko's get-rich-quick schemes, ruefully exclaims, "I knew it . . . I KNEW it!"

illusion
False perception of reality, often associated with *wishful thinking.*

Demanding more than the world can give us, we require that
something be fabricated to make up for the world's deficiency.
This is only one example of our demand for illusions.
                    —Daniel J. Boorstin, *Hidden History* (1987)

The more intelligent and cultured a man is, the more subtly he
can humbug himself.
                    —Carl Jung, *The Development of Personality* (1934)

Rob the average man of his life-illusion and you rob him of his
happiness at one stroke.
                    —Henrik Ibsen, *The Wild Duck* (1884)

impulse control
Socially desirable ability to refrain from acting on sudden wishes
or urges. Children now described as having "poor impulse control" were formerly termed "headstrong" or "unruly"; adults with
poor impulse control were once judged "reckless" or "impetuous."

in drab
Wearing clothes appropriate to one's own sex.

in drag
Wearing clothes appropriate to the other sex.

information sickness
Anxiety produced by information overload, especially from television newscasts, with their guiding programming principle, "If
it bleeds, it leads." Symptoms can include sleep disturbance, substance abuse, and *compassion fatigue.*

What's wrong with the world, I reckon, is people deliberately
courting hard luck, pressure and stress by torturing themselves

with . . . media-presented stuff they can't control themselves but that worries the hell out of them.

—Colleen McCullough,
Los Angeles Herald Examiner, May 3, 1987

Under the Nietzschean precept that what does not kill you makes you stronger, a lot of us news junkies deluded ourselves into thinking we had built up a potent immunity over the years, having been able to absorb mega-gamma rays of Grover Norquist, Larry Klayman, Alan Dershowitz, and Gerry Spence without sprouting a third ear or acquiring a twitch. But sometimes what doesn't kill you may just be setting you up for the put-away punch—which came on September 11. Since then, I've felt myself becoming info-sick for the first time, a worrywart seeing everything outlined in black, the news of anthrax and Afghanistan needlepointed into the very air, yet unable to turn off the TV, radio, computer. Sometimes I have all three going at once—while I'm reading. I've become a well-informed basket case, and I'm sure I'm not alone.

—James Wolcott, *Vanity Fair,* January 2002

Everybody gets so much information all day long that they lose their common sense.

—Gertrude Stein

See also *happy violence, mean world syndrome.*

inner child
Term coined by Baltimore therapist Dr. Charles Whitfield, author of the 1987 book *Healing the Child Within,* to describe the supposedly authentic *self,* repressed by *dysfunctional* experience. According to *pop psychology,* "getting in touch" with one's inner child is the first step toward psychological well-being.

What a distressing contrast there is between the radiant intelligence of the child and the feeble mentality of the average adult.

—Sigmund Freud

The pursuit of the Inner Child has taken over just when Americans ought to be figuring out where their Inner Adult is.

—Robert Hughes, *Culture of Complaint* (1993)

inner critic

The *perfectionist* voice inside one's head.

I write in terror. I have to talk myself into bravery with every sentence, sometimes every syllable. I have a raven perched on my right shoulder at all times that says, "That's not good, that's ugly."

—Cynthia Ozick

See also *writer's block*.

insanity

See *sanity/insanity*.

insecurity

Sense of being unsafe or not in control of one's fate. Some psychologists believe that all *neurotic* behaviors stem from it.

Wouldn't this be a great world if insecurity and desperation made us more attractive?

—Albert Brooks (as Aaron Altman) in *Broadcast News* (1987; written and directed by James L. Brooks)

insight

A perfectly good word for the grasping of some truth has been rendered loathsome by *psychobabble*.

insomnia

Chronic inability to fall asleep or to remain asleep for an adequate period of time, often caused by anxiety or pain.

> There are many nights now when I am grabbed wildly by insomnia the instant my head touches the pillow and am then tumbled about violently all night long. My body—particularly my legs, shoulders, and elbows—is heavy and unmanageable; I have no place to put them; my soul is fragile; my mind is tissue thin and easily pierced by emotions and images. I can do nothing at all. My head fills and races with disconnected thoughts. By now, I can identify this tumultuous insomnia in the first second or two; I no longer try to overcome it. It is useless. I give in to it with a sinking feeling. I lie and wait resignedly, submitting, keeping my eyes closed because that's easier, and depend on morning to come and rescue me or for sleep to steal upon me unawares after several hours and snatch me away from those buffeting cataracts of fantasy, fury, reminiscence, and speculation—that race through my head in such torrential splashes.
>
> —Joseph Heller, *Something Happened* (1974)

> Much more than time, it is sleep that is the antidote to grief. Insomnia, on the other hand, which enlarges the slightest vexation and converts it into a blow of fate, stands vigil over our wounds and keeps them from flagging.
>
> —E. M. Cioran, *Anathemas and Admirations* (1991)

> Sleep is the best of all worlds: You get to be alive *and* unconscious.
>
> —Rita Rudner

intellectual boob

Someone with a good education but no *common sense*.

infliction of emotional distress

Actionable tort in most American jurisdictions based on the relatively new idea that damages for emotional pain are recoverable at law, whether the injury was inflicted deliberately or negligently.

News Item: Two Berkeley, California, psychotherapists sued the local telephone company for $10 million in damages they claimed resulted from the cutoff of their phone service for three days. They complained that being unable to make calls caused them severe emotional distress.

Internet addiction disorder

Term coined by Ivan Goldberg in 1996 as a parody of America's obsession with addiction, but now used earnestly to describe people who are unable to control the amount of time they spend online engaging in chat rooms, auction shopping, pornography, gambling, day trading, etc.

See also *cybersex.*

Internet vampire

Someone who emerges from his computer room at dawn after a night online.

intimacy (formerly, "sexual intercourse")

The identification, acceptance, and expression of *feelings.*

> Intimacy, n. A relation into which fools are providentially drawn for their mutual destruction.
> —Ambrose Bierce, *The Devil's Dictionary* (1911)

issues

Grade-A *psychobabble* for what used to be called "problems."

J

joy
Old-fashioned word for intense pleasure or happiness.

> The secret of joy is the mastery of pain.
> —Anaïs Nin

judgment, bad
"Bad judgment" has replaced "bad behavior." Now, when caught red-handed, people (especially celebrities and public officials) confess only to exercising "bad judgment" rather than doing something wrong. (Often accompanied by the passive construction, "mistakes were made.")

judgmental
Inclined to make value judgments of other people's behavior.

> Nowadays, being ready and willing to make a decision about anything is all it takes to be called "judgmental."
> —Florence King, *National Review*, March 19, 2001

junk science
Dubious conclusions, often in the form of statistics, from pseudoscientific experiments disseminated by the popular media.

> Statistics are the lingua franca of junk science. They make good sound bites, adding a quantitative feel to otherwise "fuzzy" health scares. Credibility is added ostensibly by a statistic's neutral nature and authoritative source. The result is an inappropriate transformation of a likely meaningless number into conventional wisdom. . . .

Statistics aren't science. They may be quantitative characterizations of observations. They may be estimates from mathematical models. In either case, statistics don't explain observations or validate models. Sometimes, statistics aren't even statistics. . . .

Bad data can't produce good statistics. Never give data the benefit of the doubt. Data must earn your respect. . . .

Statistics can't prove cause-and-effect associations because they don't provide biological explanations. Without such explanations, statistical associations are hollow numbers.

—Steven J. Milloy, *Consumers' Research Magazine,* September 2001

See also *mouse terror, studies.*

K

Kafka, Franz (1883–1924)

Czech-born German-language writer of visionary fiction whose surreal, nightmarish novels (*The Trial, The Castle*) and stories ("The Metamorphosis") express the angst and alienation of modern man. The eponymous adjective "Kafkaesque" denotes injustice, frustration, and dread of some undefined but impending danger.

A lawyer by profession, Kafka was an employee of the Worker's Accident Insurance Institute of Bohemia, a job he hated but excelled at (one of only two Jews in the company, he received frequent raises and promotions). Though he wrote only as an avocation, he was a *perfectionist* who agonized over his prose.

Hypersensitive to noise, disgusted by food and its digestion (he was a vegetarian), and finding sex dirty, Kafka lived with his parents until he was thirty-one, then with one of his sisters, until he finally moved in with the woman he loved, two years before his death from tuberculosis.

The twentieth century was built largely out of absurd moments and events. In time we had to invent an adjective, European and literary, that might encapsulate the feeling of impending menace and distorted reality and the sense of a vast alienating force that presses the edges of individual choice.

These things are Kafkaesque.

—Don DeLillo, *Frontline*, November 20, 2003

I have the true feeling of myself only when I am unbearably unhappy.

—Franz Kafka

Kaminer, Wendy (1950–)
American author and social critic whose best-selling book, *I'm Dysfunctional, You're Dysfunctional: The Recovery Movement and Other Self-Help Fashions* (1992) is a lucid appraisal of the nation's obsession with victimhood and a scathing critique of the multibillion-dollar *self-help* industry.

Keaton, Diane (1946–)
American actress and director whose ditzy *persona* made her a natural for eight films with *Woody Allen*. She hemmed, hawed, and giggled her way through the acceptance speech when she won the Best Actress Oscar for her title role in *Annie Hall*, a character closely based on her.

Kinsey, Alfred (1894–1956)
American zoologist and sex researcher whose landmark book, *Sexual Behavior in the Human Male* (1948), revealed that many sex acts considered "perverted" were practiced regularly by American couples.

kleptomania
Irresistible urge to steal regardless of economic need.

Although women do most of the adult shoplifting, studies show that this is because they do most of the shopping—once in the store, men are actually more likely to take a five-finger discount. Still, the psychological dimension of such theft is classically associated with either disaffected teens or unhappy women acting out their loneliness, neglect, and feelings of emptiness.

—John Powers, *LA Weekly*, March 22–28, 2002

A kleptomaniac is a person who helps himself because he can't help himself.

—Henry Morgan

Knight, Bobby (Robert Montgomery Knight, 1940–)
Controversial American college basketball coach whose on- and off-court outbursts and ill-timed *profanity* led to his firing by the University of Indiana in 2000.
See also *adult temper tantrum, monstre sacré.*

Koren, Edward (1935–)
New Yorker cartoonist whose urban, middle-aged, middle-class characters have been aptly described by critic Don Shewey as "psychobabbling fuzzy-wuzzies."

Kraus, Karl (1874–1936)
Viennese polemicist, satirist, poet, and misanthrope. A contemporary of Freud's, he assailed middle-class values and scoffed at *psychoanalysis.*

One cleans someone else's threshold of consciousness only when one's own home is dirty.

—Karl Kraus

kvetch

(Yiddish) verb: to gripe or fret; noun: a chronic complainer, a *whiner.* Psychologists say that though kvetches enjoy the attention they get from complaining, kvetching is ultimately self-defeating because the negative emotions it generates leave them fatigued and lethargic, and may even cause stomach problems.

> It has seeped into our consciousness that complaining about life's circumstances is the normal discourse. This is an extension of everyone getting in touch with their feelings. Everyone is entitled to, but just don't tell everyone about it. Just get in touch with your feelings quietly, please.
>
> —Anthony Weiner, Brooklyn city councilman

See also *whining.*

L

Levant, Oscar (1906–1972)

American concert pianist, composer, and raconteur who appeared in Hollywood movies during the 1940s and '50s and later as a talk show personality. He was the first entertainer to discuss his psychological problems on national television, making light of his neuroses, drug addictions, and even shock treatments, at a time when such matters were considered shameful.

Born in Pittsburgh to Russian-Jewish immigrants, he believed he'd been an accident, and when asked at the age of ten what he wanted to be when he grew up, he replied, "An orphan." His mother kept him in short pants long after the other boys his age had graduated to trousers, so he started smoking to look tough. At the age of sixteen he went to New York to study piano. While playing in dance bands and giving piano lessons to support himself, he landed a role in a Broadway musical, which led to a part in the film version and a trip to Hollywood, where he met and befriended George Gershwin. Levant made numerous concert tours, playing mostly Gershwin, and he described his devotion to Gershwin's music as "a neurotic love affair."

Levant started taking sleeping pills to combat *stage fright*. In addition to caffeine and nicotine (he was a chain-smoker and drank forty cups of coffee a day) he was addicted to a variety of prescription drugs including chloral hydrate, paraldehyde, Seconal, Nembutal, and Demerol, which, he said, was "better than sex." After undergoing a series of shock treatments he wrote, "One incalculable pleasure—each shock treatment was preceded by an intravenous injection of Sodium Pentothal."

Levant had countless associative phobias based on childhood traumas, including fear of abandonment: When his parents went out in the evening, they locked him in the house alone. Once, at an outdoor Tchaikovsky concert, a sudden thunderstorm sent the audience scrambling for shelter, and young Oscar was terrified that he'd be separated from his mother. The sound of the "1812 Overture" would thereafter fill him with dread. Around the house he was called "butterfingers" for his tendency to drop things; years later the sight of a Butterfingers candy wrapper would upset him. He developed a pathological aversion to lemons after he received one as a gag prize for being the worst dancer in his high school class. He had a lifelong dread of roses after the death of a childhood sweetheart named Rose. He hated the mention of his mother's name, or of his hometown: in restaurants, the label on a Heinz ketchup bottle had to be turned away to hide the words "Pittsburgh, Pa." He dreaded the word "luck," and would almost faint if anyone wished him "Good luck!" And he couldn't bear the mention of the word "death."

Levant was also prey to countless compulsions, superstitions, and *personal rituals*. He suffered from triskaidekaphobia: he called thirteen "that terrible number" and once slept on a cot in a concert hall rather than occupy room 1301 in a Buffalo hotel.

He required all his shirts to be placed collar-front in the drawer, and always buttoned them from the bottom up and unbuttoned them from the top down. Whenever he turned on a water faucet he tapped it eight times. Before a concert he had a special pair of gloves he had to touch.

"Rituals have taken the place of religion with me," he once said, and though they may have given him a degree of comfort, they also controlled him.

An autodidact with a broad knowledge of music, literature, and sports, he read widely and voraciously and was a regular on the popular radio quiz show *Information, Please!* He switched to Lucky Strikes in 1940 when the brand became the sponsor of the show, and whenever he opened a fresh carton, he would throw away any packs that were put in "carelessly," i.e., upside down.

Levant began psychoanalysis in 1934, and was hospitalized several times over the next three decades. A psychological post-mortem declared him *bipolar* and *obsessive compulsive* with *narcissistic* personality *disorder.*

The years of drug abuse produced a severe facial tic and tremors in his hands, but couldn't dull his sharp wit: During one hospital stay he burst into the dayroom and shouted to the other patients, "Shock treatments, anyone?"

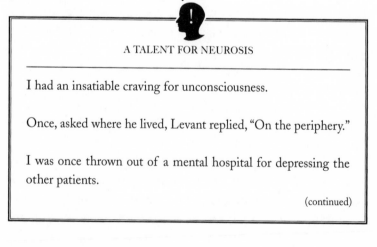

A TALENT FOR NEUROSIS

I had an insatiable craving for unconsciousness.

Once, asked where he lived, Levant replied, "On the periphery."

I was once thrown out of a mental hospital for depressing the other patients.

(continued)

I'm going to memorize your name and throw my head away!

I envy people who drink—at least they know what to blame everything on.

I could never have a mistress, because I couldn't bear to tell the story of my life all over again.

I've been unconscious for six months—I've been doing intensive research into inertia.

There is a fine line between genius and insanity, and I have erased that line.

I sleep twenty hours a day and during the other four I have the happy faculty for taking cat naps.

—Oscar Levant

Lewis, Richard (1947–)

Aka The Prince of Pain and Everyneuroticman, the quintessential neurotic actor/comedian. A self-described "bad-postured, guilt-ridden ball of confusion with a trace of paranoia, self-loathing, and a little faith thrown in for some taste," he is probably best known for self-lacerating standup routines based on his dysfunctional childhood, ineptitude at sex, and failures in relationships, for his 1989 Carnegie Hall concert, and for his dramatic turn in the film *Drunks* (1997). He originated the phrase "the BLANK from Hell" (*Bartlett's* take note) perhaps because he's been victimized by practically everything and everyone on the planet ("the mother from Hell," "the date from Hell," "the vacation from Hell"). He also single-handedly revived the archaism "mock" ("Don't mock!"). In addition to his standup work, he appears regularly on television, most notably in *Curb Your Enthusiasm* (in the role of *Larry David*'s friend "Richard Lewis") and has published a memoir, *The Other Great Depression: How I'm Overcoming, on a Daily Basis, at Least a Million Addictions and Dysfunctions and Finding a Spiritual (Sometimes) Life.*

THANK GOD YOU'RE NOT ME

When I'm touring, to keep sharp, I have problems flown in *fresh* daily.

I have a manufacturing plant of "emotional baggage" next to my house.

[I was] a dyslexic neurotic. . . . I put everyone else first, then resented it deeply, and then oftentimes ended up acting like a tremendously insensitive, self-centered jerk.

From kindergarten on, unlike Wilt Chamberlain, I've had twenty thousand rashes and *maybe* one hundred women.

During sex I fantasize that *I'm* someone else.

My family can't distinguish the real me from the performer, and when they watch me onstage, they don't realize it's a concert. There have been times when they've stood up in the audience and said, "Now Rich, we never did that."
   It's like dropping a hydrogen bomb on my timing.
   "C'mon, Uncle Phil. This is only a show. I'm kidding. You don't really have antlers."

(continued)

I quit therapy because my analyst was trying to help me behind my back.

After I got sober, I achieved so much clarity that I despise myself even more.

—Richard Lewis

lie
A deliberate falsehood.

Some mornings I wake up in a panic, because I'm convinced I've forgotten all the basics. Forgotten how to sit up, forgotten how to walk, forgotten how to talk, forgotten how to eat, forgotten how to think. Until my wife turns over and asks me a question, and I answer with my first lie of the day—and I know I'm going to make it.

—Jules Feiffer

The lie is the basic building block of good manners.

—Quentin Crisp

When you're going to lie, lie. Don't screw around.

—Dick Morris

Even a lie is a psychic fact.

—Carl Jung

It is always the best policy to tell the truth, unless of course you happen to be an exceptionally good liar.

—Jerome K. Jerome

When a person cannot deceive himself the chances are against his being able to deceive other people.

—Mark Twain

Lying is not only excusable; it is not only innocent; it is, above all, necessary and unavoidable. Without the ameliorations that it offers, life would become a mere syllogism and hence too metallic to be borne.

—H. L. Mencken

A lie is a gesture, it's a courtesy. It's a sign of respect!

—Larry David, *Curb Your Enthusiasm*

life coach
One who helps others make important decisions, sort of a personal trainer of the psyche. Not surprisingly, an occupation invented in California.

litigation
Legal proceedings to enforce a right. The United States is a particularly litigious nation because of, first, the prevailing ethos that blame can and should be placed anywhere but on the party responsible, and second, the inordinate number of lawyers, which a former Chief Justice of the United States famously characterized as hordes of hungry locusts.

Litigation, n. A machine which you go into as a pig and come out of as a sausage.

—Ambrose Bierce, *The Devil's Dictionary* (1911)

I can't put Humpty Dumpty back together again, but I can sue the bastard who pushed him off the wall.

—anonymous lawyer at a litigation seminar

For certain people after fifty, litigation takes the place of sex.

—Gore Vidal

locationship
A brief, superficial relationship based on proximity, according to Alexandra Pelosi in her documentary, *Journeys with George,* in which locationships blossom between press corps members assigned to the 2000 Bush Presidential campaign. The locationship seems to be predicated on the adage that "if you can't be with the one you love, love the one you're with."

logic
Systematic reasoning, widely decried but rarely tried, perhaps because most Americans seem to favor *feeling* over thinking.

Practically perfect people never permit thinking to muddle their sentiment.

—Mary Feelins

loner
A solitary person judged odd by nearly everyone else, even though most of the great achievements in music, art, literature, philosophy, and science result from quiet contemplation by solitary people.

Hell is other people.

—Jean-Paul Sartre, *No Exit* (1944)

One's need for loneliness is not satisfied if one sits at a table alone. There must be empty chairs as well.

—Karl Kraus

See also *quirkyalone, recluse, solitude.*

love

See *romantic love.*

lovable slob

Good person with chaotic personal habits.

> The lovable slob is a fixture in American popular culture. Neil
> Simon gave us Oscar Madison in *The Odd Couple* and Betty
> MacDonald gave us Ma Kettle in *The Egg and I.* But the slob
> alone is obnoxious. To be lovable he needs to play against his
> opposite number, the neat neurotic. Oscar's foil is peevish,
> honking Felix Unger who alienates his poker club when he
> washes the cards with ammonia; Ma Kettle's is the tight-lipped,
> disapproving Birdie Hicks, who scrubs out her henhouse with so
> much lye that she kills her hens while the Kettle hens roost in
> the parlor and flourish.
>
> The lovable slob scenario is a winner because it shows bad
> things happening to uptight people. The thing to be is a slob,
> and if you don't have a neatnik foil to make you look lovable you
> can Adopt a Spot and be your own Felix often enough to deflect
> criticism. Then you can live amid disordered piles of love, great
> gobs of feeling, and tumbling heaps of emotion in an apartment
> from Hell that is a microcosm of America—or now, a corner of
> a foreign field that is forever England.
>
>   —Florence King, *National Review,*
>   October 27, 1997

love lyrics

According to Frank Zappa (1940–1993) popular love songs
"contribute to the general aura of bad mental health in America"
because they create expectations that can never be met in real
life. In the absence of accurate information about love from any
other source (Zappa says, "Their parents don't know, so how can

they tell their kids?"), young people use lyrics to guide their behavior in relationships, often with disastrous results.
See also *wishful thinking.*

M

manic depression
See *bipolar disorder.*

manic run
Prolonged state of optimism, excitement, and hyperactivity experienced as part of *bipolar disorder.*

> When you get on a manic run, you feel like you're a house burning down from the inside out. It's like having a bellyful of electric eels. Every ball you hit is out of the park. Every word you're searching for is right at the tip of your tongue. You look through the facts in your head, your library, your catalog of memories and experiences and information, and it's all there, everything. You have every connection before you even look for it. It's the best version of yourself, sold back to yourself on the cheap every minute, every minute, every minute.
> —Carrie Fisher, *Esquire,* January 2002

marriage counseling
Talk therapy for connubial strife.

> The chief cause of unhappiness in married life is that people think that marriage is sex attraction, which takes the form of promises and hopes and happiness—a view supported by public opinion and by literature. But marriage cannot cause happiness. Instead, it is always torture, which man has to pay for satisfying his sex urge.
> —Leo Tolstoy

The horror of wedlock, the most appalling, the most loathsome of all the bonds humankind has devised for its own discomfort and degradation.

—Marquis de Sade

Passion and marriage are essentially irreconcilable. Their origins and their ends make them mutually exclusive. Their coexistence in our midst constantly raises insoluble problems, and the strife thereby engendered constitutes a persistent danger for every one of our social safeguards.

—Denis De Rougemont,
Love in the Western World (1956)

Married years are like dog years. One year of married life is like seven years of single life, because it's very compressed and concentrated.

—Larry David, *TV Guide*,
November 24–30, 2003

mask
A set of traits that disguise or conceal.

You can be a straight white male in a pinstripe suit and still have more pain than a black lesbian single mother. And that's the truth of life. People aren't willing to look beyond the masks.

—Scott Thompson

masturbation
One of the few triumphs of modern psychology has been to identify masturbation as a natural and normal human function rather than a sin or psychopathology. (Except when chicks do it.)

The best part of masturbation is the cuddling afterward.

—Woody Allen

The closest I ever came to death was when I masturbated with a 104-degree temperature.

—Larry David

As he strained at the [wine] cork . . . Billy Wilder . . . [said], "Forty-five years of masturbation and I still don't have a muscle in my hand."

—Frederic Raphael,
Eyes Wide Open: A Memoir of Stanley Kubrick (1999)

McEnroe, John (John Patrick McEnroe Jr., 1959–)

Former tennis brat whose profane, racket-smashing *adult temper tantrums* mortified traditionalists and gave license to succeeding generations of brats.

meaningful

Psychobabble for "significant."

The word meaningful when used today is nearly always meaningless.

—Paul Johnson

mean world syndrome

Term coined by George Gerbner to describe the inordinate fear of violent crime engendered by watching too much television. See also *happy violence, information sickness, television.*

melancholy

Sadness; gloom. A time-honored word lately supplanted by *depression.*

To win one's joy through struggle is better than to yield to melancholy.

—André Gide

As a confirmed melancholic, I can testify that the best and
maybe only antidote for melancholia is *action*. However, like
most melancholics, I suffer also from sloth.

—Edward Abbey

Melancholy: an appetite no misery satisfies.

—E. M. Cioran

mental hospital

A hospital for the treatment of patients with chronic *mental illness*.

Voluntary patients *think* they can leave the hospital; involuntary
patients *know* they cannot.

—Thomas Szasz, "Mental Hospital,"
The Untamed Tongue: A Dissenting Dictionary (1990)

mental illness

A psychological or behavioral *disorder* severe enough to require
psychiatric intervention. *Thomas Szasz* maintains that people
don't really have "mental illness," but rather "problems in living,"
and that psychiatric diagnoses are merely labels for human pecu-
liarities.

Mental illness is a myth, whose function is to disguise and thus
render more palatable the bitter pill of moral conflicts in human
relations.

—Thomas Szasz, *The Second Sin* (1973)

Mental illness is in the eye of the controller.

—Peter R. Breggin, *Talking Back to Prozac* (1995)

metrosexual

Urban male obsessed with his appearance, i.e., a guy who "exfoliates" religiously and uses several kinds of "hair products."

> The typical metrosexual is a young man with money to spend, living in or within easy reach of a metropolis—because that's where all the best shops, clubs, gyms and hairdressers are. He might be officially gay, straight, or bisexual, but this is utterly immaterial because he has clearly taken himself as his own love object and pleasure as his sexual preference. Particular professions, such as modeling, waiting tables, media, pop music, and, nowadays, sport, seem to attract them but, truth be told, like male vanity products and herpes, they're pretty much everywhere.
> —Mark Simpson, "Meet the Metrosexual,"
> Salon.com, July 22, 2002

See also *narcissism.*

midlife crisis

Term coined by Canadian psychoanalyst Elliot Jaques in 1965 to describe depression and anxiety about growing old in people between their late thirties and early fifties. Symptoms include regret over unfulfilled dreams, affairs with younger people, and the purchase of red sports cars. Recent research, however, including a 1999 MacArthur Foundation *study,* suggests that few people consider middle age to be a time of crisis and that the midlife crisis, though still a popular notion, may be a myth.

> We're talking midlife crisis here. I miss my youth. I've got taxes to pay, I've got hemorrhoids, I don't have any real estate, I've got kids, and they got problems, and I'm nervous about the future.
> —Abbie Hoffman

Midlife crisis is what happens when you climb to the top of the ladder and discover that it's against the wrong wall.

—Joseph Campbell

Almost every guy I know, though some of them haven't admitted it to themselves yet (most of them are successful and worked very hard to get there) it's like, when they were twenty-two they said, "What do I really, really, hate? I'm going to become *that*."

—Dave Barry, *The Portable Curmudgeon Redux* (1992)

Milgram, Stanley (1933–1984)

Controversial American social psychologist who conducted obedience experiments in which researchers in lab coats induced average people to administer ostensibly painful and dangerous electric shocks to complete strangers. The now famous experiments have come to exemplify "situationism," the power of an external situation to override conscience or temperament and make normal people behave abnormally.

mind, the

Seat of human consciousness.

The human mind is very mysterious. For example, have you ever been in a situation when you suddenly have the strange feeling that you've been in the identical situation some time in your past? Or have you ever remembered, for no apparent reason, a person or event from long, long ago? If you've had experiences like these, you're probably crazy, and you should see a psychiatrist immediately.

—Dave Barry, *Chicago Tribune*, January 20, 1985

misanthropy

Hatred or mistrust of human beings.

I never liked my own species.
>   —Gary Larsen, on why many of his *Far Side* cartoons are
>   about animals

I love mankind; it's people I can't stand.
>   —Charles M. Schulz (Charlie Brown in *Peanuts*)

What torture this life in society! Often someone is obliging
enough to offer me a light, and in order to oblige him I have to
fish a cigarette out of my pocket.
>   —Karl Kraus

It's not a particular society that seems ridiculous to me—it's
mankind.
>   —Eugene Ionesco

mishegoss
Nuttiness. According to Leo Rosten's *Joys of Yiddish*, "a wacky,
irrational, or absurd belief; a state of affairs so silly or unreal it
defies explanation; a piece of tomfoolery, clowning or 'horsing
around'; a fixation, an *idée fixe*." Connotation: *mishegoss* is almost
always used in an amused, indulgent way.

mnemophobia
See *hollow-tooth syndrome*.

modern primitives (aka "consumer tribalists")
People who tattoo, brand, or pierce their bodies.
See also *body-piercing*.

Monk, Adrian
Obsessive compulsive, multiphobic (crowds, germs, heights, dark
rooms, elevators, milk) TV detective played by Tony Shalhoub
on the popular and critically acclaimed series *Monk*. The "defective

detective" cannot abide messiness: He's compelled to straighten pictures, pick lint off suspects' clothing, and place moist towelettes on ladder rungs while following a murderer into a sewer. Monk is no mere caricature of a neurotic, but rather a complex, brilliant sleuth who, with the help of his faithful nurse/sidekick Sharona (Bitty Schram), manages to solve unsolvable crimes despite his myriad handicaps. Or perhaps because of them: clues are often apparent only to Monk precisely because of his compulsive attention to detail. According to Mr. Shalhoub, Monk has become "something of a poster boy or hero for the OCD community."

> Not to imply that I'm quite as messed up as Monk, but we all have certain things that we fixate on, and I can say that I do have my issues with stacking a dishwasher—or, rather, with the way that other people stack a dishwasher. For some reason, proper knowledge of how to stack a dishwasher has escaped the general zeitgeist, and it personally gives me great, great pleasure to stack a dishwasher in the most efficient manner, so that you fill it up and yet nothing touches anything else.
>
> —Tony Shalhoub

monstre sacré
French for "sacred monster," an insufferable celebrity whose misconduct is tolerated because of his or her charisma or talent or earning power, e.g., Roseanne, Dennis Rodman, *Bobby Knight*, Deion Sanders, Michael Jackson, Mark Cuban, Mike Tyson, *John McEnroe*, Ted Turner, Howard Stern, Roman Polanski, Barbra Streisand.

moral certainty
Conviction that one is absolutely right about religious or ethical matters.

Moral certainty is always a sign of cultural inferiority. The more uncivilized the man, the surer he is that he knows precisely what is right and what is wrong. All human progress, even in morals, has been the work of men who have doubted the current moral values, not of men who have whooped them up and tried to enforce them. The truly civilized man is always skeptical and tolerant, in this field as in all others. His culture is based on "I am not too sure."

—H. L. Mencken

The infliction of cruelty with a good conscience is a delight to moralists. That is why they invented hell.

—Bertrand Russell, *Skeptical Essays* (1928)

morale
Disused term for the state of the spirit.

Every statistic measuring well-being in the last fifty years has gone north, but measurements of morale have gone south, because people focus too much on a mood system based on daily hassles. So if you've got a hole in your swimming pool liner, you'll be just as troubled as if you're worried that the Nazis are going to come and take your child away.

—Martin Seligman, *The Washington Post*, December 24, 2002

moral indignation
Principled outrage over some ethical breach.

Moral indignation is in most cases 2 percent moral, 48 percent indignation, and 50 percent envy.

—Vittorio DeSica

Morita

Form of psychotherapy popular in Japan developed in the early twentieth century by psychiatrist Shoma Morita (1874–1938) based on the assumptions that action is preferable to reflection, that emotional problems are generated from within, and that neurosis results from too much focus on the *self*.

motivation seminar

Pricey *self-help* presentation (i.e., lecture) usually held at an airport motel. For tablecloths, add a hundred dollars.

mouse terror

Fear of potential health hazards from food additives and pesticides engendered by published experiments purporting to show harm to laboratory mice from exposure to these substances, even though the scientific validity of comparing mice to people is questionable because, first, mice aren't people, and second, exposure does not equal toxicity (i.e., dosage is everything). One such experiment concluded that "new-car smell" is toxic and another showed that dimes cause cancer (when affixed to the shaved backs of lab mice).

See also *junk science, studies.*

multiple personality disorder

Extremely rare *psychopathology* involving fragmentation into two or more distinct personalities.

> If someone with multiple personalities threatens to kill himself,
> is it considered a hostage situation?
>
> —George Carlin

Munchausen syndrome

Factitious disorder in which people feign illness, or actually make themselves sick, to get attention. Named for Baron Karl Friederich von Münchausen, an eighteenth-century German soldier known for telling tall tales about his adventures.

In one of the most extreme cases of Munchausen syndrome on record, Wendy Scott, a Scottish-born London resident, spent twelve years traveling from hospital to hospital throughout Europe, faking a variety of illnesses and undergoing forty-two unnecessary operations. Though Munchausen syndrome is considered untreatable, Miss Scott eventually recovered, and by 1999, she claimed to have lived a normal life for twenty years, attributing the cure to a pet: she had feared her cat would be neglected in her absence if she went to the hospital. Miss Scott counseled other Munchausen victims until her health genuinely began to fail. Ironically, she was refused treatment in Britain because of her history. She went to the United States, where she was diagnosed with advanced intestinal cancer, and died soon thereafter, at the age of fifty.

Munchausen syndrome by proxy
Parent makes own child sick so parent can get attention. Gambits include poisoning, suffocation, starvation, intentionally overdosing the child's medication, falsifying medical charts, and tampering with IV drips or feeding machines.

Muzak
Soothing music piped into public venues.

> Born in elevators and supermarkets, Muzak has spread to restaurants, hotels, airplanes, telephone hold services, and waiting rooms. The public-relations experts believe that human beings fear silence—that is, the absence of constantly imposed direction. It is further believed that if we can be relieved of our fears, we will gain enough self-confidence to buy, eat, vote, fly, or simply go on living.
> —John Ralston Saul, *The Doubter's Companion* (1994)

myth of the modem, the
The *rationalization* that cybersex isn't cheating on one's spouse or significant other because there's no physical contact involved.

Myth of Sisyphus, the
Sisyphus was condemned by Zeus to push a huge boulder up a steep hill forever. Every time the boulder neared the top it would roll back down and Sisyphus would have to start all over again, i.e., an apt metaphor for the *human condition*.

> The struggle to reach the top is itself enough to fulfill the heart of man. One must believe that Sisyphus is happy.
>
> —Albert Camus, *The Myth of Sisyphus* (1942)

N

nanny envy
1. Resentment of your nanny because of all the time she spends with your children when you can't. 2. Envy of your friends who can afford a nanny when you can't.

narcissism
Excessive admiration of oneself, often coupled with the need for constant flattery. People who were once judged "egotistical," "conceited," or "vain" are now called "narcissistic." The term derives from Narcissus, a handsome youth in Greek mythology who, unable to tear himself away from his own reflection in a pool, wasted away and died.

There's a distinction between what might be called benign narcissists, those who have a healthy sense of their accomplishments and who like praise but don't crave it, and malignant narcissists, who may seem confident on the surface but who actually feel worthless inside, are hypersensitive to any slights or imagined insults, and sink into depression and anger if they don't receive constant adulation.

What psychoanalysts term "narcissistic vulnerabilities" make malignant narcissists especially sensitive to the way other people regard them, though they lack *empathy* for others. Malignant narcissists are hard to treat because they resent any challenge to their inflated self-image and thus have difficulty bonding with a therapist. Narcissism is often an underlying problem in patients with other problems (depression, failed relationships). In extreme cases it can lead to such criminal conduct as stalking, murder, and even terrorism.

> Simple narcissism gives the power of beasts to politicians, professional wrestlers, and female movie stars.
> —Norman Mailer, "Miami and the Siege of Chicago" (1968)

> He decocts matters of the first philosophical magnitude from an examination of his own ordure, and I am not talking about his books.
> —William F. Buckley of Norman Mailer

> I've never looked forward to a birthday like I'm looking forward to my new daughter's birthday, because two days after that is when I can apply for reinstatement.
> —Pete Rose

> DICK SCHAAP: What did you think about while you were on suspension?
> REGGIE JACKSON: The magnitude of *me*.

> I love my life.
> —Julia Roberts, presenting the Best Actor Award at the 2002 Academy Awards, upon opening the envelope and learning that Denzel Washington had won

We're all here for the same reason: to love me.

—Barry Manilow, to a concert audience

One of my chief regrets during my years in the theater is that I couldn't sit in the audience and watch me.

—John Barrymore

There were some initial difficulties when the director first told me the disappointing news that if the film was to have any semblance of reality at all there would have to be moments when other people were on screen at the same time I was.

—Bette Midler

I was the smartest, best-looking, most charismatic of the underbosses who flipped.

—Salvatore "Sammy the Bull" Gravano

To be engrossed by something outside ourselves is a powerful antidote for the rational mind, the mind that so frequently has its head up its own ass—seeing things in such a narrow and darkly narcissistic way that it presents a colorectal theology, offering hope to no one.

—Anne Lamott, *Bird by Bird* (1994)

Is a narcissist's suicide a crime of passion?

—Howard Ogden, *Pensamentoes, Volume II* (2003)

Celebrities—athletes, politicians, movie stars—are especially prone to *narcissism*. (Are they narcissists because they're celebrities, or are they celebrities because they're narcissists?) Some stars demand to be photographed only from what they deem their "best" side. Others go to hideous lengths to create a distinctive "look": Marlene Dietrich had her upper rear molars extracted to create her trademark sunken cheeks; Clark Gable had all his teeth pulled and a set of dentures installed when he arrived in Hollywood (Vivien Leigh would complain of the odor while making *Gone with the Wind*); Merle Oberon refused to smile for fear of causing wrinkles and plucked her hairline to create a perfect oval visage. In a switch on the usual celebrity rhinoplasty, Judy Garland wore a latex prosthesis to actually enlarge her nose.

And, of course, hairpieces are ubiquitous. Male celebrities garnish their crania with all manner of fake fur:

> Charlton Heston wears a hairpiece. His character in *A Man for All Seasons* was bald. Instead of doing without his hairpiece, he put a bald pate *over* it.
>
> —Dustin Hoffman

For his televised eightieth birthday celebration, Frank Sinatra wore a $2,500, top-of-the-line hairpiece—a gift from Joseph Paris, a New York hairdresser who has looked after Ol' Blue Eyes' pate for years.

Like thirty-five million other Americans, Sinatra has male-pattern baldness. He had hair transplants about twenty-five years ago, said Paris, who made his first hairpiece for Sinatra in 1980, to wear in the film *The First Deadly Sin*. Frank's new "rug" is made of a material like nylon, with each strand of synthetic hair sewn on individually. "A man of eighty shouldn't have a massive amount of hair," said Paris, who noted that the colors of Sinatra's hairpiece were custom blended, with several shades of silver-gray—lighter for the hairline and temples, darkest for the back, and a combination on the sides. The singer was so pleased, he had Paris flown to his Beverly Hills home to cut and style it for the TV special, shown in December. After the show, he ordered a second hairpiece. (It takes two

months to make.) At home, said Paris, Sinatra relaxes without
any headgear.

—*Parade Magazine*

See also *acquired situational narcissism, delusions of grandeur.*

national character
Supposed set of traits unique to a given nation.

National character is only another name for the particular form
which the littleness, perversity, and baseness of mankind take in
every country. Every nation mocks other nations, and all are
right.

—Arthur Schopenhauer

What is the difference between heaven and hell? the wise man
was asked. In heaven, he replied, the English are the police, the
French are the cooks, the Italians are the lovers, the Swiss are
the administrators, and the Germans are the mechanics.
Whereas in hell, the English are the cooks, the French are the
administrators, the Italians are the mechanics, the Swiss are the
lovers, and the Germans are the police.

—Anonymous

That's the trouble with you Americans: You expect nothing
bad ever to happen, when the rest of the world expects only
bad to happen. And they are not disappointed. You have
everything, and still you complain. You lie on couches, bitch to
your psychiatrists. You got too much time to think about your-
selves.

—Svetlana Kirilenko (Alla Kliouka)
to Tony Soprano (James Gandolfini)
in *The Sopranos,* "The Strong, Silent Type"

neatnik
Gratuitous pejorative for an orderly person. When a neatnik tells you he can't go out because he has to rearrange his sock drawer, it isn't just an excuse.

needs
What we believe we require for physical or emotional health. Usage note: Often combined with "my" but rarely with "your."

nervous breakdown
Term now considered too vague to be of clinical value, but which remains popular with the general public to describe emotional and physical incapacitation accompanied by deep depression. To "have a nervous breakdown" is to cease functioning and withdraw, to snap under severe pressure, to suffer a wrenching break from life. In a survey released in 2000, about a third of Americans said they have felt on the verge of a nervous breakdown at least once.

The list of famous people who've had nervous breakdowns includes F. Scott Fitzgerald, who documented his in *The Crack-Up* ("Every act of life from the morning tooth-brush to the friend at dinner had become an effort"), Philip Roth, William Styron, Mike Wallace, Art Buchwald, Kitty Dukakis, Margot Kidder, and the late Rod Steiger, who said about the experience, "You don't shave. You don't shower, you don't brush your teeth. You don't care."

> One of the symptoms of an approaching nervous breakdown is the belief that one's work is terribly important.
> —Bertrand Russell

See also *neurasthenia*.

neurasthenia

Nervous exhaustion and related symptoms first identified in 1869 and originally named "American nervousness" because it was thought to be caused by the stress of nineteenth-century American life. Among notable neurasthenics were Edith Wharton, Alice James, Elizabeth Barrett Browning, and Dr. Margaret Cleaves, author of *Autobiography of a Neurasthene* (1886), who called the condition "sprained brain." The standard treatment was a "rest cure" in which the neurasthenic was confined to bed for up to six months.

See also *antique diagnosis, nervous breakdown.*

neurosis

General term for a range of mild mental *disorders* (some would say "quirks") characterized by anxiety, depression, or compulsive or phobic behavior, all with no apparent physical cause. Literally "nerve disorder," the word was coined in the late eighteenth century by the Scottish physician William Cullen to characterize nervous symptoms with no organic origin.

Freud believed that neurosis results from unresolved sexual conflicts during the first six years of life: The child never fully recovers from parental restrictions on the infantile sexual drive, causing anxiety that manifests in the form of neurotic behavior in adulthood. Others trace neurosis to the assertion of parental authority in order to socialize the child, which breaks the child's will, dampens his spontaneity, and ultimately results in psychological damage when the child replaces his true self with a pseudoself to appease his parents (and, indirectly, society). The child's subsequent interpersonal experiences are clouded by these early psychological scars. In another view, neurosis takes the place of religious ritual for those who lack the gift of faith, and there is even some research linking certain neuroses to a specific gene.

The symptoms of neurosis . . . are essentially substitute gratification for unfulfilled sexual wishes.

—Sigmund Freud

Neurosis is a substitute for legitimate suffering.

—Carl Jung

Work and love—these are the basics. Without them there is neurosis.

—Theodore Reik, *Of Love and Lust* (1957)

Neurosis involves issues of style, not substance. It's a kind of escapism for the well-off individualist.

—Hillel Schwartz

My definition of neurosis is spending too much time trying to correct a wrong.

—Gene Wilder

Everyone has flaws. It's a matter of finding the ones you can live with.

—Moon Unit Zappa

I prefer neurotic people. I like to hear rumbling beneath the surface.

—Stephen Sondheim

The only people for me are the mad ones, the ones who are mad to live, mad to talk, mad to be saved, desirous of everything at the same time, the ones who never yawn or say a commonplace thing, but burn, burn like fabulous yellow Roman candles.

—Jack Kerouac

The poet is in command of his fantasy, while it is exactly the mark of the neurotic that he is possessed by his fantasy.

—Lionel Trilling, *The Liberal Imagination* (1950)

neurotic guilt
Guilt based on emotional disquiet rather than actual wrongdoing.

neurotic need
Need arising from some emotional imbalance.

Americans have a neurotic need not to be neurotic.

—Florence King

neurotic/psychotic
What's the difference between neurosis and psychosis? Is it a matter of degree? Is it a question of thinking versus behavior? What distinguishes, say, the "baby blues" (mild postpartum depression experienced by a significant percentage of recent mothers) from the homicidal postpartum depression of Andrea Yates, the Houston woman who in 2002 calmly drowned her five children? The defining feature seems to be that neurotics have a firmer grip on reality than psychotics, and that neurotics are able to function normally. More or less.

Neurotic means he is not as sensible as I am, and psychotic means he's even worse than my brother-in-law.

—Karl Menninger

Those who suffer from and complain of their own behavior are usually classified as "neurotic"; those whose behavior makes others suffer, and about whom others complain, are usually classified as "psychotic."

—Thomas Szasz

All neurotics are petty bourgeois. Madmen are the aristocrats of mental illness.

—Mary McCarthy, *The Group* (1963)

A neurotic builds castles in the air; a psychotic not only builds them but also lives in them.

—Richard Casement,
"Man Suddenly Sees the Edge of the Universe"

Neurotics build castles in the air, psychotics live in them. My mother cleans them.

—Rita Rudner

New Age
Pertaining to the spiritual and consciousness-raising movements of the 1970s and '80s, including such disparate elements as ecology, organic food, trance-channeling, crystals, and holistic medicine.

Hello seeker! Now don't feel alone here in the New Age, because there's a seeker born every minute.

—Firesign Theatre

Newyorkitis
Term coined by James Girdner in his 1901 book of the same name to describe the "haste, rudeness, restlessness, arrogance, contemptuousness, excitability, anxiety, pursuit of novelty and of grandeur, pretensions of omniscience, and therefore prescience" of New Yorkers.

I had to move to New York for health reasons. I'm very paranoid and New York is the only place where my fears are justified.

—Anita Wise

When you're neurotic in New York, it means you have a link to
being an intellectual. And it also often means there's a charm
and depth to your feelings.

—Sondra Farganis, sociology professor at the New School for
Social Research

At the deli in my building [in Manhattan], there are always two
people working at the cash register. One takes your money while
the other puts your food in a bag. The whole transaction happens in less time than it takes to get your pocket picked. Instead
of the customers losing patience with waiting "on line," as they
say here, it is the cashiers who seem annoyed that the customers
can't get their change into their wallets and get out of the way
fast enough.

—Rick Newman, *The Washington Post,* September 9, 2001

There's an interesting survey in the current *Journal of Abnormal
Psychology:* New York City has a higher percentage of people
you shouldn't make any sudden moves around than any other
city in the world.

—David Letterman

niche worrying
Sharply focused anxiety.

Niche worrying is a means of conveniently organizing one's
paranoia. It's concentrating on a specific fear or phobia at an appropriate time, like focusing on getting Legionnaires' disease
from inhaling steam containing *Legionella pneumophila* bacteria
while taking a shower at the gym.

—Cameron Tuttle, *The New York Times,* July 13, 1997

nihilism

1. Philosophical doctrine that nothing really exists; 2. the *delusion* that the *self* does not exist.

See also *solipsism*.

> The unrest which keeps the never stopping clock of meta-
> physics going is the thought that the nonexistence of this world
> is just as possible as its existence.
> —William James, *Essays in Radical Empiricism* (1912)

Nixon, Richard Milhous (1913–1994) (aka "Tricky Dick")

Thirty-seventh president of the United States (1969–1974). Though he achieved "détente" with the U.S.S.R., ended U.S. military involvement in Vietnam, and visited China, he is best remembered for having been the first U.S. president to resign the office.

According to biographer Anthony Summers in *The Arrogance of Power: The Secret World of Richard Nixon* (2000), President Nixon was diagnosed "neurotic" by a psychotherapist and medicated himself with the anticonvulsant prescription drug Dilantin to relieve depression caused by public outrage over U.S. bombing of Cambodia in 1970. And, according to Summers, in 1974, while under the pressure of the Watergate investigation, Nixon's mental state so deteriorated that U.S. secretary of defense James Schlesinger commanded all military units not to respond to orders from the White House unless they were cleared with him or the secretary of state.

> People have got to know whether or not their president is a
> crook. Well, I'm not a crook.
> —Richard M. Nixon, press conference, November 11, 1973

> What starts the process really are laughs and slights and snubs
> when you are a kid. . . . But if you are reasonably intelligent and
> if your anger is deep enough and strong enough, you learn that

you can change those attitudes by excellence, personal gut performance, while those who have everything are sitting on their
fat butts.

—Richard M. Nixon,
quoted by Tom Wicker in *One of Us* (1991)

nocebo

Latin for "I will harm"; a negative *placebo;* physical manifestation
of pessimism; self-fulfilling prophecy of disbelief. In the nocebo
effect, a bad result occurs with no physiological basis. Media
programming that encourages fear of disease may be a factor
(see *information sickness*). In one *study,* women who believed they
were prone to heart disease were four times more likely to die of
it than women with the same risk factors but without a pessimistic outlook. In another experiment, subjects cautioned
about possible gastrointestinal side effects from aspirin were
three times as likely to suffer them as those who received no
such warning. Perhaps the ultimate manifestation of the nocebo
effect is voodoo death, in which the victim actually dies after an
"evil spell" is put on him.
See also *placebo.*

normal

Conforming with a norm, standard, or pattern; regular, natural,
typical. For example, in one society (e.g., the United States) it
might be considered more or less normal to pierce the nose and
tongue as a form of decoration, while the same practice would
be deemed barbaric or primitive in another society (e.g.,
Afghanistan).

I told the doctor I was overtired, anxiety-ridden, compulsively
active, constantly depressed, with recurring fits of paranoia.
Turns out I'm normal.

—Jules Feiffer

The only normal people are the ones you don't know very well.

—Joe Ancis, *New York* magazine

Nobody realizes that some people expend tremendous energy
merely to be normal.

—Albert Camus

I can't cure normal.

—Laura Schlessinger

nymphomania
Immoderate sexual desire in a female, a term rendered obsolete
by the sexual revolution.

O

obesity
Condition of being overweight measured against prescribed
weight ranges according to age and height. Once seen as a character flaw, obesity is now deemed a behavioral *disorder.*

The one way to get thin is to reestablish a purpose in life. . . .
Obesity is a mental state, a disease brought on by boredom and
disappointment.

—Cyril Connolly, *The Unquiet Grave* (1944)

See also *eating disorder.*

obsessive-compulsive disorder (OCD)
Relentless repetition of a feeling or action in an attempt to assuage guilt or relieve anxiety caused by recurrent intrusive
thoughts or images. Though frequent hand-washing, repeated

checking of locks, touching of certain objects, and other *personal rituals* do relieve tension, they hamper OCD sufferers in their daily activities. Some are so self-conscious about their behavior, which they know is odd but cannot control, that they withdraw from society completely. Some researchers believe OCD is biochemical and hence treatable with medication.

In a *New Yorker* cartoon, a little girl being read a bedtime story asks her father, "Is the Itsy Bitsy Spider obsessive-compulsive?"

Checklist to identify obsessive-compulsive disorder:

1. Do you need to check the same things more than three or four times?

2. Do you obsess with thoughts of sex or violence without acting on them?

3. Do you have the same thoughts over and over without being able to get rid of them?

4. Do you avoid contact with things that appear as if they could be contaminated although other people don't avoid these things?

5. Do you wash your hands more than two or three times [in one session]?

6. Do you take an abnormal amount of time completing tasks because they have to be exact?

7. Do you sometimes think that if you don't do something, harm will come to someone else?

—Laura Saari, *The Orange County Register,* April 3, 1991

Is checking a checklist to identify obsessive-compulsive disorder itself a symptom of obsessive-compulsive disorder?

—Howard Ogden

I would clean a bathroom that hadn't been used, just because I had a schedule of things that I did every day. I even washed my keys and my checkbook. . . .

If someone came into my house and went to open something, especially things that were closed, it was almost like they were touching my insides or something. It was bad enough if they touched something that was lying on a table, but if someone went to open something, like a drawer or a closet, it felt like I was being molested. I work as a volunteer for a rape crisis center. The way rape victims describe how they feel when they've been raped is how I would feel.

—Fran Sydney, founding member of the
Obsessive-Compulsive Disorder Foundation,
Chicago Tribune, February 26, 1989

Oedipus complex

According to *Freud*, Boy lusts after Mother, which makes Boy want to murder Father, which in turn causes Anxiety. Boy fails to cope with Anxiety and violà: *Neurosis*. Most contemporary authorities scoff at this twisted fairy tale.

offsetting behavior

Human tendency to do something harmful or dangerous because attendant risks have been reduced, as when drivers drive faster because their cars are equipped with airbags and antilock brakes, or when heart patients feel free to indulge in rich foods because they're on cholesterol-lowering medication.

olfactory reference syndrome (ORS)

Obsessive, irrational fear that one's body emits an unpleasant odor despite frequent showering and repeated use of deodorant, perfume, and mouthwash. Some ORS sufferers believe the imagined odor causes others to cough, sneeze, or turn away, and in extreme cases they quit their jobs and withdraw from society to avoid embarrassment.

oppositional defiant disorder

According to columnist Michael Skube, the inability to take *psychobabble* seriously.

optimism/pessimism

Tendency to expect the best/worst.

> Optimist, *n.* A proponent of the doctrine that black is white.
> —Ambrose Bierce, *The Devil's Dictionary* (1911)

> Optimism is the folly of maintaining that everything is all right when we are wretched.
> —Voltaire, *Candide* (1759)

> When encouraged as a social attitude it [optimism] is an infantalizing force which removes the individual's conscious power to criticize, refuse and doubt. Optimism, like patriotism, is the public tool of scoundrels and ideologues.
> —John Ralston Saul, *The Doubter's Companion* (1994)

> The optimist proclaims that we live in the best of all possible worlds; the pessimist fears this is true.
> —James Branch Cabell, *The Silver Stallion* (1928)

I'm a recovering optimist.

—Larry Gelbart

I find nothing more depressing than optimism.

—Paul Fussell

The basis of optimism is sheer terror.

—Oscar Wilde

There is nothing sadder than a young pessimist.

—Mark Twain

A pessimist is a person who has had to listen to too many optimists.

—Don Marquis

Do you know what a pessimist is? A person who thinks everybody is as nasty as himself and hates them for it.

—George Bernard Shaw

The man who is a pessimist before forty-eight knows too much; if he is an optimist after it, he knows too little.

—Mark Twain

All pessimists keep two sets of books, and in one of them they believe something great will happen.

—David Brown

Pessimism of the intellect, optimism of the will.

—Quoted by Edward Said as his motto,
Charlie Rose, October 7, 1999

In spite of everything, I still believe that people are really good
at heart.

> —Anne Frank, shortly before being
> sent to her death in a concentration camp

See also *defensive pessimism.*

order panic disorder
Fear of menus; inability to deal with the decisions involved
when eating in restaurants, according to *Los Angeles Times* writer
Paul Brownfield, a self-proclaimed sufferer who needs to know
what other people at the table are having before he can make a
choice.

> A few decades of research has made it clear that most people
> are terrible choosers—they don't know what they want, and the
> prospect of deciding often causes not just jitters but something
> like anguish. The evidence is all around us, from restaurant-
> goers' complaints that "the menu is too long" to Michael Jack-
> son's face.
>
> > —Christopher Caldwell,
> > *The New Yorker*, March 1, 2004

Othello delusion
Groundless suspicion that one's sexual partner is unfaithful.
See also *delusion, delusions of grandeur.*

Othello effect
Theory advanced by psychologist Paul Ekman describing what
can occur in an interview or interrogation when a person who is
actually truthful may feel so anxious that he won't be believed by
the interrogator (a police officer, for instance) that he acts ner-

vous, as if he has something to hide, which in turn causes the interrogator to doubt his truthfulness.

outing
Practice of publicly revealing someone's hidden homosexuality.

> Why is being outed such a big deal? When I find out that
> someone's gay, my respect for them increases tenfold.
> —Scott Thompson, *The Kids in the Hall*

out-of-body experience
Putative flights of the spirit while the body stays home.

> Out-of-body experiences are out-of-mind experiences.
> —James Randi, *Larry King Live*

P

panic
Sudden, overwhelming fear.

> Sometimes at the peak of intoxicating pleasures, I am visited by
> a panic: the phone or doorbell will ring, someone will need me
> or demand that I do something. Of course I needn't answer or
> oblige, but that is beside the point. The spell will have been bro-
> ken. In fact the spell has already been broken. The panic itself is
> the interruption. I have interrupted myself. Oddly enough, very
> often the phone does ring, just as paranoiacs can have enemies.
> Life is designed to thwart ecstasy; whether we do it for our-
> selves or something does it for us is a minor issue.
> —Lynne Sharon Schwartz, *Ruined by Reading* (1997)

panic attack (formerly "spell")
Brief episode of sudden, overpowering anxiety with no apparent cause, coupled with such physical symptoms as dizziness, nausea, chest pains, or elevated heart rate.
See also *Soprano, Tony.*

parapraxis
See *Freudian slip.*

parenting
Done properly, the time-consuming, exhausting practice of raising children through love, guidance, and concern.

> They fuck you up, your mum and dad.
>   They may not mean to, but they do.
> They fill you up with faults they had
>   And add some extra just for you.
>
> —Philip Larkin,
> "This Be the Verse," *High Windows* (1974)

> The first half of our lives is ruined by our parents, and the second half by our children.
>
> —Clarence Darrow

> My parents did not want me. They put a live teddy bear in my crib.
>
> —Woody Allen

> My parents only had one argument in forty-five years. It lasted forty-three years.
>
> —Cathy Ladman

> No woman can shake off her mother.
>   —George Bernard Shaw, *Too True to Be Good* (1934)

A Jewish man with parents alive is a fifteen-year-old boy and
will remain a fifteen-year-old boy till they die.
—Philip Roth, *Portnoy's Complaint* (1969)

To make a child in your own image is a capital crime, for your
image is not worth repeating. The child knows this and you
know it. Consequently you hate each other.
—Karl Shapiro, *The Bourgeois Poet* (1964)

No wire hangers!
—Joan Crawford to her adopted daughter,
quoted by Cristina Crawford in
Mommie Dearest (1978)

paranoia

Technically, a severely psychotic *disorder* characterized by *delusions* of persecution; colloquially, a common form of anxiety.

Paranoia, or more exactly the adjective *paranoid,* was debased in
the 1960s by young people who used it in disparagement of
everyone who was anxious about anything, which meant almost
all of us. That our anxiety was quite reasonable was considered
irrelevant, *irrelevant* being another word that they rendered void
by indiscriminate use.

Nowadays, anyone who has the slightest fear about anything
is labeled paranoid. If I am afraid that when I leave my new car
in a supermarket parking lot somebody will open his door and
ding it, I am paranoid. This happened to me just the other
night.
—Jack Smith, "I'm Paranoid, You're Paranoid"

I am not paranoid, and if you write that I am paranoid, I will
personally sue the *New York Times*.
—Rex Reed, letter to the *New York Times*

I envy paranoids; they actually feel people are paying attention
to them.

—Susan Sontag

Just because you're paranoid doesn't mean the bastards aren't out
to get you.

—Lorenz Hart

Peanuts
Popular comic strip by Charles M. Schulz (1922–2000) featur-
ing a bunch of *neurotics* disguised as children.

peeping tom
One who gets pleasure from furtively watching others, named
for Peeping Tom of Coventry, a tailor in eleventh-century England who was struck blind for being the only one to see Lady
Godiva naked. We've come far.

Pekar, Harvey (1939–)
OCD sufferer, clutterer, math-anxiety victim, lifelong Cleveland
resident, and, as author of the graphic novel *American Splendor*,
practitioner of unflinching realism. Also known for fractious in-
terviews with David Letterman.

Ordinary life is pretty complex stuff.
—Harvey Pekar, from the subtitle to *American Splendor* (2003)

penis envy
Freud's theory that the greatest force shaping the female psyche
is the unconscious desire for a penis was long the basis of perceived male superiority, at least before the advent of strap-ons.

In this society, the norm of masculinity is phallic aggression.
Male sexuality is, by definition, intensely and rigidly phallic. A

man's identity is located in his conception of himself as the pos-
sessor of a phallus; a man's worth is located in his pride in phallic identity. The main characteristic of phallic identity is that
worth is entirely contingent on the possession of a phallus.
Since men have no other criteria for worth, no other notion of
identity, those who do not have phalluses are not recognized as
fully human.

—Andrea Dworkin, *Our Blood* (1976)

Women don't suffer from penis envy, *men* do.

They are such fractional parts of the total construction they
might easily be overlooked if we did not dwell on them. They
are arrogant and absurd in their haughty, sniffing, pushy, egotistical pretensions. (We let them get away with an awful lot.)
They can't even hold their lordly pose for half a day a week.
What a feeble weapon indeed for establishing male supremacy, a
flabby, collapsing channel for a universal power drive ejaculated
now and then in sporadic spoonfuls. No wonder we have to
make fists and raise our voices at the kitchen table.

—Joseph Heller, *Something Happened* (1974)

people pleaser (formerly "good egg")

Someone so desperate for approval that he or she can't say no, always puts the needs of others first, rarely does anything for him-
or herself, and feels guilty when he or she does.

I get extremely nervous in sales situations. I will do absolutely
anything to please the salesperson. Usually, in stores, I can flee
on foot before a salesperson gets to me, but if I don't get away,
I'm a dead man. Like, if I'm walking through Sears, and I happen to pause for just a moment in the major appliances section,
and one of those Sears appliance salespersons in polyester sports
jackets comes sliding up and says, "Can I help you?" I instantly
go into a state of extreme anxiety and say, "Yes, I'll take one of

these, please," pointing to whatever major appliance I happen to be standing in front of, even though we probably already have one.

—Dave Barry

There's no one nastier than a recovering people-pleaser.

—Howard Ogden, *Pensamentoes, Volume II* (2003)

See also *codependency*.

perfectionism
Belief that professional, moral, or social perfection is both desirable and attainable, a notion once taken for granted but now deemed unrealistic and self-defeating by *pop psychology*, so that being labeled a "perfectionist" has become an accusation rather than a compliment.

I think [perfectionism] is a good thing. I think it's terrific. I want my brain surgeon to be a perfectionist. I want my mechanic to be a perfectionist. I think we are in such a love-of-mediocrity society that we can't tolerate anybody who really desires excellence. . . . Every gifted person I've met is a perfectionist. They are driven to attain very high standards. Without that we would not have Olympic champions, we would not have great art, great books wouldn't be written.

—Linda Silverman, psychologist

The indefatigable pursuit of an unattainable perfection, even though it consist in nothing more than the pounding of an old piano, is alone what gives meaning to our life on this unavailing star.

—Logan Pearsall Smith, *Afterthoughts* (1931)

See also *control freak*.

persona

Contrived public image or role. Movie stars depend on their personae to transcend any given "vehicle," i.e., they play themselves in movie after movie and don't really act, but rather "behave" as their persona would behave in the situation. Hence John Wayne's indomitable Westerner, Jimmy Cagney's likable tough guy, Jack Nicholson's leering hipster, Cary Grant's suave sophisticate.

> I figured I needed a gimmick, so I dreamed up the drawl, the squint, and a way of moving which meant to suggest that I wasn't looking for trouble but would just as soon throw a bottle at your head as not.
>
> —John Wayne

> I invented Cary Grant, and then I became him.
>
> —Cary Grant

See also *Rita Hayworth syndrome.*

personality

Collective psychological traits of an individual, including temperament, emotions, and intelligence.

> Creative powers can just as easily turn out to be destructive. It rests solely with the moral personality whether they apply themselves to good things or to bad. And if this is lacking, no teacher can supply it or take its place.
>
> —Carl Jung

> Personality is the supreme realization of the innate idiosyncrasy of a living being. It is an act of high courage flung in the face of life.
>
> —Carl Jung

personality test
Standardized psychological test designed to evaluate a subject's *personality*.

> In September, I finally started work on *State Fair*, and though I had tested for the part of Margy, the chaste farm girl, I was re-cast as Emily, the bad girl, a switch based on my personality test.
> —Ann-Margret, *My Story* (1994)

personal ritual
Repetitive, usually private acts or procedures performed to relieve stress.

> Do you wait for the phone to ring at least twice before answering even if it's right beside you?
> How many times do you check the knobs on your stove to make sure they're off before you leave the house?
> And when you're at a newsstand and you flip through a magazine and you decide to buy that magazine, do you reach for another copy because the one you were flipping through is no longer new?
> Some idiosyncrasies you might be somewhat embarrassed about, others you claim sole ownership to because of their ingeniousness. People will either think of you fondly because of them or it will irk the hell out of them and they won't want anything to do with you. Let's face it, they're what make you, you. . . . But the bottom line is: *nobody's playing with a full deck.*
> —Judy Reiser,
> *And I Thought I Was Crazy!* (2001)

See also *obsessive-compulsive disorder.*

perverse
Disposed to error or fault; contrary; unnatural; kinky.

The heart *prefers* to move against the grain of circumstance;
perversity is the soul's very life.

—John Updike, "More Love in the Western World"

pessimism
See *optimism/pessimism*.

phallic symbol
More Freudian filth: Everything long and pointy is supposed to
be reminiscent of a phallus. But, *Freud* was a confirmed cigar
smoker. When asked by a student whether his cigars were sym-
bolic objects, Freud replied, "Sometimes a cigar is just a cigar."

pharmacracy state
Thomas Szasz's term for a society where "all sorts of human
problems are transformed into diseases and the rule of law ex-
tends into the rule of medicine." In a pharmacracy state, medical
controls replace legal and religious authority.

Inasmuch as we have words to describe medicine as a healing
art, but have none to describe it as a method of social control or
political rule, we must first give it a name. I propose that we call
it pharmacracy, from the Greek roots *pharmakon*, for "medicine"
or "drug," and *kratein*, for "to rule" or "to control." . . . As theoc-
racy is rule by God or priests, and democracy is rule by the people or the majority, so pharmacracy is rule by medicine or
physicians.

—Thomas Szasz, *Ceremonial Chemistry:
The Ritual Persecution of Drugs, Addicts, and Pushers* (1974)

phobia
An intense, irrational, often disabling fear. By some estimates,
one in five Americans suffers from at least one phobia, and new
phobias are being identified (or at least named) all the time:

NINETEEN PHOBIAS YOU'VE NEVER HEARD OF

aeronausiphobia	fear of vomiting from airsickness
anuptaphobia	fear of being single
arachibutyrophobia	fear of peanut butter getting stuck to the roof of the mouth
automatonophobia	fear of ventriloquist's dummies
blennophobia	fear of slime
cherophobia	fear of gaiety
ephebiphobia	fear of teenagers
euphobia	fear of good news
defecaloesiophobia	fear of painful bowel movements
dismorphobia	fear that a body part is misshapen
heterophobia	fear of straight people
kyphophobia	fear of stooping
macrophobia	fear of waiting
metrophobia	fear of poetry
oneirogmophobia	fear of wet dreams
pediophobia	fear of dolls
pentheraphobia	fear of one's mother-in-law
syngenesophobia	fear of relatives
xanthophobia	fear of the color yellow

Tell us your phobias, and we will tell you what you are afraid of.
—Robert Benchley

If there were such a thing as phobophobia—the fear of developing a phobia—might it not be induced by watching a TV talk show on which phobics discuss their fears? Or maybe the alternate reaction would occur in some viewers: They would become fearful because they had no unreasonable fears and worry that there was nothing in their lives interesting enough to be worthy of a TV talk show.

—Tom Shales, *Chicago Tribune,* April 16, 1985

I'm scared of electricity. Every time I plug something in, I think I'm going to die.

—John Waters

All of us are born with a set of instinctive fears—of falling, of the dark, of lobsters, of falling on lobsters in the dark, of speaking before a Rotary Club, and of the words "Some Assembly Required."

—Dave Barry

I'm scared to death of being stone cold sober.

—Jerry Lee Lewis

I have an irrational fear of snakes. When my husband and I moved to a part of Los Angeles County with many rattlesnakes, I tried to desensitize myself by driving every day to a place called Hermosa Reptile Import-Export and forcing myself to watch the anacondas. This seemed to work, but a few years later, when we were living in Malibu and I had a Corvette, a king snake (a "good" snake, not poisonous, by no means anaconda-like) dropped from a garage rafter into the car. My daughter, then four, brought it to show me. I am ashamed to say I ran away. I still think about what would have happened had I driven to the market and noticed my passenger, the snake, on the Pacific Coast Highway.

—Joan Didion

I hyperventilate opening a box of chocolates. I'm the most nervous guy in the world, a frightened little man on red alert from when I wake up until I go to sleep. I was born with fear.

—Ozzy Osbourne

I have this terrible fear that I'm going to be forced to take a general knowledge test in public.

—Dick Cavett, *The Tonight Show*, June 20, 1979

I have a horror of sunsets. They are so romantic, so operatic.

—Marcel Proust

I am petrified of bikini waxing. I had a very bad experience in 1978.

—Arnold Schwarzenegger

I am scared easily, here is a list of my adrenaline production: 1. small children, 2. policemen, 3. high places, 4. that my next movie will not be as good as the last one.

—Alfred Hitchcock

Avoiding danger is no safer in the long run than outright exposure. The fearful are caught as often as the bold.

—Helen Keller

We have nothing to fear but fear itself.

—Franklin Delano Roosevelt, inaugural address (1933)

The British poet Philip Larkin managed to combine microphobia (fear of germs) and xenophobia (fear of foreigners) in a single sentence:

I'm afraid I always feel London is very unhealthy—I can hear fat Caribbean germs pattering after me in the Underground.

—Philip Larkin

placebo
Inert agent, e.g., sugar pill, that produces a positive physiological effect ("placebo" is Latin for "I shall please"). The placebo is be-

lieved to trigger the body's inherent healing mechanism: Physicians have long observed that if a patient believes in a remedy, the results tend to be positive, even if the remedy is a sham. Decades of *studies* indicate that placebos alleviate symptoms in from 10 to 70 percent of patients, and that the color of a pill influences its effectiveness: Red or pink pills are stimulants, large blue pills sedatives, and small yellow pills antidepressants. However, current research has exposed the placebo effect as a medical myth: A Danish study analyzing 114 clinical trials found that patients who received no treatment at all improved at the same rate as those who got placebos.

> Can placebos cause side effects? If so, are the side effects real?
> —George Carlin

See also *nocebo*.

plastic surgery addiction
Disorder in which the addict must have more and more "work" (breast augmentation, liposuction, fat grafting, collagen or Botox injections) done to obtain the desired rush of reassurance. These "slaves of the scalpel," according to *Mademoiselle* contributor Jill Neimark, are "caught in the same cycle of elation and despair one finds in obsessive dieters or bodybuilders."

> Centuries from now, when an archaeologist digs up our civilization, he'll find dust, bones, and a collection of implant bags.
> —Brian Novack, plastic surgeon

> We can make better breasts than God.
> —Maja Ruetschi, plastic surgeon

> One popular new plastic surgery technique is called lipgrafting, or "fat recycling," wherein fat cells are removed from one part of

your body that is too large, such as your buttocks, and injected
into your lips; people will then be literally kissing your ass.

—Dave Barry

I liked Michael Jackson better dark. And I liked his nose a lot
better, too. If he has any more stuff taken off, I don't know how
he's gonna breathe.

—Loretta Lynn, *Esquire*, January 2002

It is now rare in certain social enclaves to see a woman over the
age of thirty-five with the ability to look angry.

—Alex Kuczynski,
The New York Times, February 7, 2002

What does it profit a seventy-eight-year-old woman to sit
around the pool in a bikini if she cannot feed herself?

—Erma Bombeck

plutomania
Pathological desire for wealth.
See also *affluenza*.

political correctness
The apotheosis of mediocrity; the unholy union of conformity
and hypocrisy; the substitution of one form of bigotry with another; a national epidemic of *euphemism* transmitted by media,
public institutions, and pressure groups that outlaws any language or behavior that might possibly be construed as offensive
to anyone, anywhere, at any time.

Being politically correct means always having to say you're sorry.

—Charles Osgood

At the meeting, the senate voted to approve a mural to be placed in the commons. There was some concern voiced by the senate about the contents of the mural.

"I see some pilgrim invaders here," said Elisa Haro, academic affairs director. "It kind of reminds me of my colonization, and I don't like that."

The artist of the mural said that the pilgrim invaders were meant to be Shakespearean actors and that he would try to make that more clear.

Other concerns with the mural included the depiction of white cranes, which the senate demanded be changed to colored cranes.

They were also concerned with the lack of a same-sex couple depicted, which the artist agreed to add. The senate voted to approve the mural in the light of the adjustments being made.

> —Minutes of the May 2003 meeting of the Associated
> Students of the University of California, Riverside

What this country needs is less political correctness and more grammatical correctness.

> —Howard Ogden, *Pensamentoes, Volume II* (2003)

POLITICALLY CORRECT PHRASES

The attempt to avoid offending anyone has produced terminology that should offend everyone.

act out (misbehave)

aurally challenged (hard of hearing)

(continued)

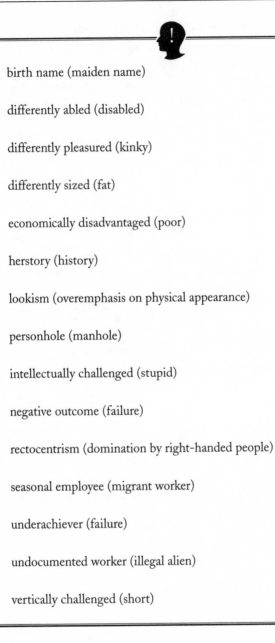

birth name (maiden name)

differently abled (disabled)

differently pleasured (kinky)

differently sized (fat)

economically disadvantaged (poor)

herstory (history)

lookism (overemphasis on physical appearance)

personhole (manhole)

intellectually challenged (stupid)

negative outcome (failure)

rectocentrism (domination by right-handed people)

seasonal employee (migrant worker)

underachiever (failure)

undocumented worker (illegal alien)

vertically challenged (short)

See also *victim mentality*.

polymorphously perverse
Having omnidirectional sexual tendencies, i.e., oral, anal, and masturbatory, a propensity of infants and rock stars.

pop psychology
Popular misconceptions masquerading as conventional wisdom. These psychology myths and half-truths, widely disseminated by *self-help* books and media therapists, now saturate everyday discourse.

THE FIVE MYTHS OF POP PSYCHOLOGY

1. Human beings are basically good.

2. We need more self-esteem.

3. You can't love others until you love yourself.

4. You shouldn't judge anyone.

5. All guilt is bad.

—Chris Thurman, *Self-Help or Self-Destruction* (1982)

See also *psychobabble, self-help*.

profanity
Vulgar or abusive language.

> Under certain circumstances, profanity provides a relief denied even to prayer.
>
> —Mark Twain

pronoia
The irrational belief that people like you.

Prozac
Brand name for fluoxetine hydrochloride, an antidepressant widely used in the treatment of moderate depression. Prozac has been heralded as a wonder drug in spite of questions about side effects: Many patients complain that the drug puts up a "wall" between themselves and their feelings, and there is mounting evidence linking it to suicide.

> [Being on Prozac] is not at all like being on cruise control. It's more like driving a car with an unreliable fuel gauge on a long trip on an unfamiliar highway with no signs to indicate the distance to the next gas station or rest stop—and not minding.
> —Sally Halprin, "Life with Prozac,"
> *San Francisco Sunday Examiner & Chronicle*, August 15, 1993

Prozac defense
In 1991, Palm Beach, Florida, housewife Kathy Willets (aka "The Palm Beach Nympho") pleaded guilty to prostitution, but with an explanation: Prozac had induced the *nymphomania* that made her operate a brothel in her home. After serving four hundred hours of community service, she continued her sex career, both as an adult film star (she appeared in a dozen films, including *Naked Scandal*, which tells her life story) and as an "attraction" at the Bunnyranch in Nevada.

psychiatry
Quasi-medical discipline that diagnoses and treats mental and emotional *disorders*. The public image of psychiatry has been damaged by the almost total discrediting of *Freud*, by negative portrayals of psychiatrists in movies and on television, and by

revelations of the sexual misconduct and financial impropri-
eties of prominent psychiatrists. When a national survey dis-
closed that almost 10 percent of U.S. psychiatrists have had
sexual contact with their patients, *The American Journal of
Psychiatry* strongly urged those doctors to seek help (presum-
ably from psychiatrists who avoid sexual contact with their
patients).

Unlike physical disease, most psychological problems cannot be
attributed to any known physiological pathology. Although we
can safely assume that psychological problems are related to the
central nervous system, the fact is that we know very little about
the biological basis for schizophrenia, even less about anxiety
and depression, and virtually nothing about the physiological
causes of personality disorders.
>   —G. E. Zuriff, clinical psychologist, "Medicalizing
>   Character," *The Public Interest*, spring 1996

All too often, a [psychiatric] diagnosis is little more than an educated guess, and sometimes it's not that educated.
>   —Michael Skube, *The Atlanta Journal-Constitution*,
>   March 24, 1998

Anyone who goes to a psychiatrist ought to have his head exam-
ined.
>   —Samuel Goldwyn

Psychiatry enables us to correct our faults by confessing our parents' shortcomings.
>   —Laurence J. Peter

I suspect that our own faith in psychiatry will seem as touchingly quaint to the future as our grandparents' belief in phrenology seems now to us.

—Gore Vidal

A psychiatrist is a man who goes to the Folies Bergère and looks at the audience.

—Mervyn Stockwood

Why should I tolerate a perfect stranger at the bedside of my mind?

—Vladimir Nabokov, *Strong Opinions* (1973)

Mental health is too important to leave to the psychiatrists.

—Howard Ogden, *Pensamentoes, Volume II* (2003)

psychoanalysis (aka "the talking cure")

Therapy originated by *Sigmund Freud* and others which seeks to elicit repressed thoughts in order to resolve hidden conflicts supposedly at the root of personality *disorders*. Once or twice a week for many years, the patient comes to the analyst's office, lies on a couch, and says everything that comes to mind. As the patient talks, aspects of his unconscious emerge, which the analyst refines and redirects (through the use of such techniques as *free association* and *dream interpretation*) in order to provide the patient with *insights,* which help him eliminate undesirable behaviors or debilitating symptoms.

Freud is the father of psychoanalysis. It has no mother.

—Germaine Greer

Psychoanalysis is confession without absolution.

—G. K. Chesterton

Psychoanalysis is the mental illness it purports to cure . . . the occupation of lascivious rationalists who reduce everything in the world to sexual causes, with the exception of their occupation.

—Karl Kraus

Let the credulous and the vulgar continue to believe that all mental woes can be cured by a daily application of old Greek myths to their private parts.

—Vladimir Nabokov

Acting is the expression of a neurotic impulse. It's a bum's life. The principal benefit acting has afforded me is the money to pay for my psychoanalysis.

—Marlon Brando

I once asked Woody Allen how his psychoanalysis was going after twenty-five years. He said, "Slowly."

—John Cleese

I've always felt this about psychoanalysis: I'm a bad clarinet player, and I once brought my clarinet in to have it overhauled because the pads were getting rotten and the springs were no good. The guy did a beautiful job, and I came back and said to him, "Will I play better now?" And he said, "Yes, but not as much as you'd like to." That's the exact same thing with psychoanalysis. One hopes it's going to solve all your problems, and it doesn't really solve any of them, but it does help.

—Woody Allen

I'm spending about $600 a week talking to my analyst. I guess that's the price of success.

—Robert De Niro

It is a common delusion that you make things better by talking about them.

—Rose Macaulay

The man who once cursed his fate, now curses himself—and pays his psychoanalyst.

—John W. Gardner, *No Easy Victories* (1968)

psychoanalyst

Title usually applied to a psychiatrist trained in psychoanalysis, though the term is not protected by state or federal law and hence anyone may use it.

pyschobabble

Term coined by social critic Richard Dean Rosen to describe psychiatric jargon used indiscriminately. Psychobabble reduces the *human condition* to a few catchwords and "conceals what it claims to reveal," according to Theodore Dalrymple. The use of pseudoscientific jargon by nonprofessionals was once considered bad manners, and armchair diagnosis would provoke the challenge, "Who made *you* a psychiatrist?" upon which the abashed offender would shut up. No more. Now we routinely encapsulate our friends and relatives with glib diagnoses, and preadolescents describe their peers in terms found in the *DSM* ("I'm like, he's so *anal!*").

Psychobabble is . . . a set of repetitive verbal formalities that kills off the very spontaneity, candor, and understanding it pretends to promote. It's an idiom that reduces psychological insight to a collection of standardized observations, that provides a frozen lexicon to deal with an infinite variety of problems.

—Richard Dean Rosen,
*Psychobabble: Fast Talk and Quick Cure
in the Era of Feeling* (1977)

We have a whole new language, which gives some people the illusion, I suppose, that we have a whole new range of experiences. We no longer simply know people or are acquainted with people or sleep with people or are married to people; we have *relationships* with people. If two people are giving anything of themselves to each other, they are said to be making *commitments;* and if they do this for any length of time, they are said to be having an *ongoing* relationship.

If it is ongoing long enough and the commitments are deep enough, they are said to be having a *meaningful* relationship.

If any children result from such a relationship, the partners to it go into a phase called *parenting,* and if they are conscientious and supportive, they are known as *caring.*

With no connections or responsibilities to any other person it is possible to be known as a *caring* person just by feigning a caring manner when someone else is in a jam. How often we hear it said, "He's a very caring person," of some curmudgeon who has neither wife nor dog. . . .

Human nature hasn't changed much since Chaucer and Shakespeare, and while our institutions have changed greatly, we are just beginning to deal with the fact that men beat their wives and adults abuse children and ongoing relationships are no more meaningful than ever.

—Jack Smith, "Most Unique in La La Land"

I have never been a fan of personality-conflict burgers and identity-crisis omelets with patchouli oil. I function very well on a diet that consists of Chicken Catastrophe and Eggs Overwhelming and a tall, cool, Janitor-in-a-Drum. I like to walk out of a restaurant with enough gas to open a Mobil station.

—Tom Waits

Psychobabble is a mindset that can cause otherwise intelligent people to say ridiculous things:

> The main reason for the tremendous popularity of football in America may be our subconscious fascination over the fact that each play starts with the quarterback squatting between the center's legs in the classic pose of sodomy.
>
> —Norman Mailer

WARNING: People who pretend to scoff at psychobabble are sometimes the worst offenders.

See also *oppositional defiant disorder, pop psychology.*

psychobiography
Posthumous *psychoanalysis* of a celebrity or historical figure, thus:

Leonardo da Vinci was a latent homosexual who had an intense erotic attachment to his mother.

John Adams, vain, ambitious, obstinate, was America's most neurotic Founding Father, and probably borderline *bipolar.*

Casanova wasn't just a libertine; having been abandoned early by his mother, he lived to please women and genuinely cared for his conquests.

Abraham Lincoln entered politics literally to get out of the house, preferring the campaign trail to frequent abuse at the hands of Mary Todd Lincoln, who regularly struck him in the face and threw things at him.

Charles Darwin suffered from *panic disorder* caused by anxiety that his theory of evolution would be ridiculed by the British scientific establishment.

Adolf Hitler was narcissistic, compulsive, phobic, and obsessed with the thought that his paternal grandfather was Jewish (Hitler also hated his looks and thought his nose "looked Jewish").

Joseph Stalin had low *self-esteem* and an enemy complex.

Sammy Davis Jr. secretly wanted to be white, hence the faux British accent and conversion to Judaism (see also *anglolalia*).

psychological phlegm
Buried feelings that need to be expressed, as in, "The therapy's really going well—I've been bringing up a lot of psychological phlegm!"

psychology
Ostensibly scientific study of human behavior in the attempt to explain, influence, and predict future behavior.

That psychology is simple mumbo jumbo—as laughable in its practice as shamans foretelling futures by casting bones on the sand—would not be worth pointing out if so many people did not believe in it. . . .

The once-reasonable study of the mind and its ways has calcified into a whole field of certainties and beliefs every bit as rigid as the interpretation of Creation by a Bible Belt preacher.

—Bill Granger, *Chicago Tribune*,
November 22, 1987

Psychology wants to know what a man's problems are; character has to do with how he surmounts them.

—Joseph Epstein,
Partial Payments (1989)

It seems a pity that psychology has destroyed all our knowledge
of human nature.
                              —G. K. Chesterton, *The London Observer*,
                                                December 9, 1934

See also *pop psychology*.

psychopathology
A psychological *disorder;* the study and classification of same.

psychosis
Severe mental *disorder* characterized by lack of contact with real-
ity.
See also *neurotic, psychotic*.

psychosomatic
Relating to a physical illness with a psychological cause. See also
hypochondria.

psychotherapy
Generic term for any situation involving a trained professional
and an individual seeking help for mental or emotional problems.

There is a profound tension . . . between psychotherapy as a
business that needs to retain its customers and psychotherapy as
a practice that has the health of its patients at heart.
                              —Lauren Slater, *The New York Times Magazine*,
                                                February 3, 2002

When I was in therapy about two years ago, one day I noticed
that I hadn't had any children. And I like children at a distance.
I wondered if I'd like them up close. I wondered why I didn't

have any. I wondered if it was a mistake, or if I'd done it on purpose, or what. And I noticed my therapist didn't have any children either. He had pictures of his cats on the wall. Framed.

—Spalding Gray, *Swimming to Cambodia: The Collected Works of Spalding Gray* (1985)

Q

quarterlife crisis (aka "midtwenties breakdown")
Feelings of confusion and self-doubt experienced by people in their twenties, especially after completing their education.

A period of mental collapse occurring in one's twenties, often caused by an inability to function outside of school or structured environments, coupled with a realization of one's essential aloneness in the world. Often marks induction into the ritual of pharmaceutical usage.

—Douglas Coupland, *Generation X* (1991)

See also *midlife crisis.*

queen bee
A socially savvy alpha girl who ruthlessly spreads gossip and dictates to other girls how they should act, what they should wear, and with whom they should associate, all in an effort to maintain her pack-leader status.
See also *relational aggression.*

quiet desperation
Mute resignation to a life blighted by the grinding conformity of postindustrial society.

The mass of men lead lives of quiet desperation. What is called
resignation is confirmed desperation.

—Henry David Thoreau, *Walden* (1854)

Nowadays most men lead lives of noisy desperation.

—James Thurber, "The Grizzly and the Gadgets" (1956)

quiet loner
A *loner* with a gun.

quirkyalone
One who claims to enjoy being single, at least until Mr. or Ms.
Right comes along.

When I eventually met Mr. Right I had no idea that his first
name was Always.

—Rita Rudner

R

rage
Intense, explosive anger that sometimes leads to random violence.
Specific forms of rage emerging over the last two decades include
road rage, runway rage (the result of long ground delays), and Little
League rage (aka "rink rage," "soccer rage," "sideline rage"), a growing phenomenon at children's sporting events: Parents, trying to
live vicariously through their children, many of whom have little or
no interest in the sport, are harassing coaches and officials in record
numbers. The problem has gotten so bad that more and more
leagues and municipalities are requiring parents to sign codes of
conduct before allowing them to participate. (See also *adult temper
tantrum.*) But these well-publicized rages are only the rim of the
volcano, and new rages are being identified all the time:

THE NEW RAGES

Dot.com Rage
Anger and disappointment at the commercialization of the Internet.

Snow Rage
Adults pulling guns on children for throwing snowballs.

Spam Rage
Man threatens to kill employees of company he claims clogged his e-mailbox with unwanted messages.

Cell-Phone Rage
Backlash to exposure to *secondhand speech. Hang up and drive! (Walk! Shop!) You're not that important!*

Hold-Music Rage
If I must be on terminal hold, *please:* Just leave me alone with my thoughts.

AWOL-at-the-Register Rage
You were in front of me in the checkout line a minute ago, but now you've gone to get another item, leaving me, the others in the line, and the cashier in checkout limbo. You should be tried and convicted in absentia and sentenced to roam the aisles forever!

Shopping-Cart Rage
A broken wheel keeps spinning around, the cart is impossible to steer, and *I can't take it anymore!*

(continued)

Take-a-Number Rage

I've waited patiently at the bakery counter for my number, 23, to be called. When 22 is finally announced and nobody answers, I shout a silent *finally!* to myself. Then I hear the magic "23," but before I can part my lips to form the word "here," from the back of the crowd comes a breathless, "I've got 22!" This woman had been "double dipping," i.e., she had taken a number and then disappeared to do other shopping (while I waited at the counter like a fool). *Justifiable homicide!*

Salad-Bar Rage

Hel-*lo:* It isn't "finger food," you e-coli-spreading swine!

More-than-Ten-Items Rage

The world full of sociopaths!

Divider Rage

The person ahead of me is already being rung up but I can't start loading my items onto the belt because, *aiyeeee, there's no divider!*

Clueless-at-the-Register Rage

What, you didn't know you'd have to *pay*? You thought maybe they were *giving* the stuff away?

Voice-Mail Rage

I've got your "Your call is important to us" right here!

Cellophane Rage

Why should you need a scalpel to unwrap a CD?

(continued)

Cable Rage
Two hundred channels and *still* nothing on!

Catalog-Copy Rage
If I have to read about one more product made of a fabric that "wicks away moisture," I'm going to kill someone.

Tattoo Rage
Why do you do that to yourself? You think that's *attractive?*

Oversized SUV Rage
Gashole!

Bank-Line Rage
I didn't know you could refinance your mortgage at the teller window!

Ponytail Rage
Face it, dude, you're bald!

People-Who-Make-Little-Quote-Marks-with-Their-Fingers Rage
You need to be "punished." With "extreme prejudice."

Rage Rage
WHY AM I SO $@#*&%#@*&$@ ANGRY ALL THE TIME?!

Road rage, air rage. Why should I be forced to divide my rage into separate categories? To me, it's just one big, all-around, everyday rage. I don't have time for fine distinctions. I'm busy screaming at people.

—George Carlin

I'm a rage-aholic. I'm addicted to rage-ahol.

—Homer Simpson

See also *road rage, roid rage.*

railway neurosis
Upon their introduction in the mid-nineteenth century, trains induced severe stress in a population that had never traveled faster than a horse could gallop. People were terrified and over-whelmed by the size and power of the new machines, and there were frequent accidents. Injured passengers began to sue for "concussion of the spine" or "railway spine," a purported physical injury diagnosed as "inflammation of the spinal membranes" with symptoms of confusion, anxiety, and insomnia. As rail-roads were held increasingly liable by the courts, they contrived to shift the emphasis from railway spine, a supposed physical in-jury, to "railway neurosis," a psychological trauma, because they'd be required to pay less in damages for "distress of mind" than for bodily harm. Railway neurosis was thus the first coupling of the stresses of modern life with what is now called *neurosis,* the first acknowledged psychosomatic illness, and a tacit validation of the emerging discipline that would be known as *psychotherapy.* (Sigmund Freud characteristically attributed his own terror of trains to a childhood rail trip during which he saw his mother undressed.)
See also *tücke des objekts, die.*

rationality
Quality of being logical.

> Rational, adj. Devoid of all delusions save those of observation,
> experience and reflection.
> —Ambrose Bierce, *The Devil's Dictionary* (1911)

rationalization
According to *psychoanalytic* theory, the process of ascribing false
reasons for one's behavior in order to justify or conceal one's true
motivation.
See also *self-delusion*.

reality
That which actually exists, despite *wishful thinking* and other efforts to the contrary.

> I refuse to be intimidated by reality anymore. After all, what is
> reality but a collective hunch?
> —Jane Wagner, *The Search for Signs of Intelligent Life in the*
> *Universe* (1986)

> Reality is a staircase going neither up nor down, we don't move,
> today is today, always is today.
> —Octavio Paz, "The Endless Instant"

> Our *now* is so brief and instantaneous that we don't have a sense
> of solidity that I assume we once had. The world used to consist
> of big blocks of solid stuff. And the world today seems to con-
> sist of squirming fractal bits.
> —William Gibson, "Disneyland with the Death Penalty"

> What was once called the objective world is a sort of Rorschach
> ink blot, into which each culture, each type of personality, reads

a meaning only remotely derived from the shape and color of
the blot itself.

—Lewis Mumford, *The Conduct of Life* (1951)

Reality is that which, when you stop believing in it, doesn't go
away.

—Philip K. Dick, *I Hope I Shall Arrive Soon* (1985)

Reality is for people who can't face drugs.

—Laurence J. Peter, *Peter's People* (1979)

Human kind
Cannot bear very much reality.

—T. S. Eliot, "Burnt Norton," *Four Quartets* (1943)

reality television

Unscripted programming in which real people in artificially dangerous or embarrassing situations compete for money or prizes.

Reality on TV is hardly new: Frederick Wiseman, Allen Funt,
and the Loud Family of PBS fame, to name a few, have several
reels to show you. But reality on TV (human behavior largely
unaffected by awareness of a camera) and reality TV have almost nothing in common. To be fair, reality TV doesn't claim to
be about everyday life. Instead, it's pitched as the pursuit of
dreams (money, love, stardom, Darwinian anointment). But even
that's not real (you should pardon the expression). The new
shows aren't about empowerment and fantasy fulfillment.
They're about humiliation. They worship at the altar of degradation, the altar of deception, the altar of letting people attempt
things that they have no talent for.

—Andrew Postman, *The Washington Post,*
February 23, 2003

The Amish don't have as good a lobbying group.
—CBS CEO Leslie Moonves, announcing a new reality series in
which Amish teenagers leave their insular community for the
big city. Moonves was alluding to the network's abandonment
of another series based on the 1960s sitcom *The Beverly Hillbillies*
after intense criticism from a lobbying group called the
Center for Rural Strategies.

reasonable people
Rational human beings. Possibly an oxymoron.

Reasonable people adapt themselves to the world. Unreasonable
people attempt to adapt the world to themselves. All progress,
therefore, depends on unreasonable people.
—George Bernard Shaw

recluse
One who shuns the world to live in seclusion. Most recluses are
either homeless, independently wealthy, or artists, because it's
hard to pursue a career if you won't leave the house. In rare cases
(Thomas Pynchon, *J. D. Salinger, Howard Hughes*) reclusiveness
can be a useful PR strategy.

The world is always curious, and people become valuable merely
for their inaccessibility.
—F. Scott Fitzgerald

Prestige cannot exist without mystery, for one reveres not what
one knows well.
—Charles de Gaulle

See also *agoraphobia; Hughes, Howard; loner; solitude.*

recovery movement

Approach to addiction treatment based on the ideology that we are all diseased and incapable of controlling our behavior without the help of a *support group.*

Exaggerating every foible, bad habit and complaint, taking our behavior out of our control and defining us as adult children, recovery encourages invalidism. Calling the recovery process self-help doesn't change the way it tends to disempower people.

It is an odd program in self-esteem that rewards people for calling themselves helpless, childish, addicted and diseased and punishes them for claiming to be healthy. Admit that you're sick, and you're welcomed into the recovering persons fold; dispute it and you're "in denial." Thus the search for identity is perversely resolved: all your bad behaviors and unwanted feelings become conditions of your being. Instead of a person who smokes, you are a nicotine addict. Instead of a person who is sometimes depressed, you are a sadness addict. (Feelings can be addictive, too, we're told.) . . .

The phenomenal success of the recovery movement reflects two simple truths that emerge in adolescents: all people love to talk about themselves, and most people are mad at their parents. You don't have to be in denial to doubt that truths like these will set us free.

—Wendy Kaminer, *I'm Dysfunctional, You're Dysfunctional: The Recovery Movement and Other Self-Help Fashions* (1992)

redemption

What was once distinctly religious, i.e., salvation from a state of sin, is now a secular sacrament for public transgressors such as, for example, Jayson Blair, the *New York Times* reporter caught plagiarizing from other reporters and fabricating stories. After his firing from the *Times,* Blair appeared on the cover of

Newsweek and published a book in which he excused himself as a victim of racism, childhood sexual abuse, and manic depression.

> Who says America loves retribution? We threw away those scarlet letters decades ago; now it's redemption that sells. Even better, that redemption is near-painless and near-instantaneous. From Oliver North to Monica Lewinsky to Lizzie Grubman, the media are filled with former miscreants. The cameras are always ready and eager to tell the miscreants' story, record their contrition, highlight their comeback.
> —Maria Puente, *USA Today*, May 22, 2003

reduced consumerism
See *conspicuous austerity.*

reductionism
The attempt to explain complex phenomena with basic principles, as by attributing mental acts to the operation of chemical and physical laws.

> "You," your joys and your sorrows, your memories and your ambitions, your sense of personal identity and free will, are in fact no more than the behavior of a vast assembly of nerve cells and their associated molecules.
> —Francis Crick, *The Astonishing Hypothesis: The Scientific Search for the Soul* (1993)

> Incredible shame is associated with mental illness. People will confide the most intimate details of their love life before they'll mention a relative who has had a serious mental breakdown. But the brain is just another organ. It's just a machine, and a machine can go wrong.
> —Candace Pert, neuroscientist

I am not a mechanism, an assembly of various sections. And it
is not because the mechanism is working wrongly, that I am ill.
I am ill because of wounds to the soul.

—D. H. Lawrence

rehabilitation ("rehab")

Medically supervised, institutionalized treatment of addiction.
Before the advent of the Betty Ford Clinic in Rancho Mirage,
California, and other rehab facilities, celebrity addicts and alcoholics, if they did anything at all, would go to a sanitarium to
quietly "dry out." Now they publicize their substance abuse to
"help others."

Rehab? The first time is a gift. The second time is a bitch.

—Carrie Fisher, *Esquire*, January 2002

Elizabeth Taylor has been in Betty Ford more than Gerald
Ford.

—Bill Maher

relational aggression

Constellation of catty behavior, including ridicule, ostracism,
gossip-mongering, and even body language, whereby adolescent
girls vent their mutual hostilities. The phenomenon has been
documented in Rosalind Wiseman's *Queen Bees and Wannabes*
and Rachel Simmons's *Odd Girl Out. Studies* have shown that
teenage females, though less physically aggressive than males,
are more socially aware, and they use that savvy to covertly but
ruthlessly jockey for pack position.

One Australian researcher, Laurence Owens, found that the
fifteen-year-old girls he interviewed about their girl-pack pre-
dation were bestirred primarily by its entertainment value. The

girls treated their own lives like the soaps, hoarding drama, constantly rehashing trivia. Owens's studies contain some of the more vivid anecdotes in the earnest academic literature on relational aggression. His subjects tell him about ingenious tactics like leaving the following message on a girl's answering machine—"Hello, it's me. Have you gotten your pregnancy test back yet?"—knowing that her parents will be the first to hear it. They talk about standing in "huddles" and giving other girls "deaths"—stares of withering condescension—and of calling one another "dyke," "slut," and "fat" and of enlisting boys to do their dirty work.

—Margaret Talbot, *The New York Times Magazine,*
February 24, 2002

ELAINE: Why do they call it a "wedgie"?

GEORGE: Because the underwear is pulled up from the back until . . . it wedges in.

JERRY: They also have an Atomic Wedgie. Now the goal there is to actually get the waistband on top of the head. It's very rare.

ELAINE: Boys are sick.

GEORGE: What do girls do?

ELAINE: We just tease someone until they develop an eating disorder.

Seinfeld, "The Library"

See also *queen bee.*

relationship

Template of interplay between people based on blood, kinship, or affinity.

The word *relationship* best refers to the connection between parasite and host, or shark and remora.

—Ian Shoales

Also, a Hollywood euphemism for a business association:

> It's not about cars, it's about *relationships*. . . . What we were try-
> ing to do is say, "Thank you for being so special to us."
> —Sherry Lansing, a Paramount Pictures executive, explaining why
> the studio bought Mercedes-Benz convertibles for Tom Cruise,
> Sidney Pollack, and the producers of *The Firm* (1993).

repression
According to *Freud,* the unconscious exclusion of painful thoughts
or feelings.

> People are very secretive—secret even from themselves.
> —John Le Carré, *The London Observer*, December 31, 1985

> God wouldn't have given us repression if he hadn't wanted us to
> use it.
> —Toni Grant, psychologist

resentment
Ill will over real or imagined grievances.

> Resentment is like taking poison and waiting for the other per-
> son to die.
> —Carrie Fisher

retail therapy
Shopping as a means of comfort, relaxation, or mood elevation,
or to mask emotional problems; merchandise as medication. *Retail therapy* can range from the palliative novelty of buying a new
handbag, to the purchase of useless items from QVC, to the attempt to buy your way into the future, as when an ambitious
young executive buys a car he can't afford hoping it will enhance

his prospects for promotion to a higher-paying job (which will allow him to afford the car).

> Because you see the main thing today is—shopping. Years ago a person, if he was unhappy, didn't know what to do with himself—he'd go to church, start a revolution—something. Today you're unhappy? Can't figure it out? What is the salvation? Go shopping.
>
> —Arthur Miller, *The Price* (1968)

> If you are tired of shopping you are going to the wrong shops.
>
> —Wallis, Duchess of Windsor,
> *The London Times*, June 18, 1994

See also *compulsive shopping disorder.*

retirement panic
Fear of not having enough money for retirement (especially prevalent among baby boomers).
See also *studies.*

retrospectoscope
Those wags who like to say that "hindsight is 20/20" have gone high-tech.

Rita Hayworth syndrome
Confusion of image and reality. Early in 2002, the actress Kim Cattrall, who played the insatiable Samantha on the HBO series *Sex and the City,* published a sex manual she said she was "compelled to write" (with her then husband, Mark Levinson) by "two entire, long, awful decades of bad sex" caused by what she termed "the Rita Hayworth syndrome," i.e., the men she dated confused her with the characters she played in films, including

the foul-mouthed gym coach in *Porky's* (1982), while in reality the characters were nothing like her. The term refers to the life of Rita Hayworth, the pinup girl and movie sex goddess whose series of husbands and lovers (including Victor Mature, Orson Welles, Ali Khan, and Dick Haymes) never produced a lasting relationship.

> Men go to bed with Gilda, but wake up with me.
>
> —Rita Hayworth

See also *persona.*

Ritalin (methylphenidate hydrochloride)

Stimulant prescribed—some say overprescribed—for children diagnosed with *Attention-Deficit/Hyperactivity Disorder (ADHD).* The only real problem many children deemed disruptive may have is that they are children, but they're nevertheless dosed with Ritalin simply to reduce inconvenience to the educational system and, not incidentally, to their own parents. Some *studies* indicate that three or four times as many children are on Ritalin than need be.

There have been several class-action lawsuits charging the drug's manufacturer, the Swiss drug company Novartis AG, and the American Psychiatric Association with conspiring to fraudulently promote the use of Ritalin and misrepresenting the severity of its side effects, which include insomnia, loss of appetite, and cardiovascular and central-nervous-system problems.

> We may not know all of the medical consequences [of giving schoolchildren Ritalin] for another twenty or thirty years. In social terms, it gives the impression to people that behavioral problems are medical and should be handled with drugs; it imposes a certain stigma on the child, possibly on the family. It medicalizes educational and childrearing problems, and it may

cause biological problems in the person taking the drug. I don't know if the average person on Main Street realizes that if a thirty-year-old man has a pocketful of Ritalin, he can go to jail for years. This is called "speed." And this is what they give as a treatment to schoolchildren when there's absolutely no laboratory or medical evidence that they are sick.

—Thomas Szasz, "Curing the Therapeutic State"

The epidemic of ADD cases is only the most visible example of the impulse to pathologize more or less ordinary behavior. There are classrooms in which half the students are on Ritalin. Kids are diagnosed and labeled if they're not "on-task," teacher-talk for behaving like little soldiers, and they're diagnosed if they concentrate too well. I know of a twelve-year-old girl who will read contentedly for hours. The teacher thinks something's wrong and told the parents she thinks their daughter has ADD. We should at least be honest and call these children patients. By one recent study, fully one-fourth of the students in the nation's public schools have a "learning disability." As you might expect, federal money plays a part. When the Individuals with Disabilities Education Act went into effect in 1976, most schoolchildren it covered were physically impaired in some way. Less than one-quarter had learning disabilities. By 1992, those with learning disabilities represented 52 percent—2,369,385 disabled children—with more than $1 billion in federal money going to schools for programs to teach them.

—Michael Skube, *The Atlanta Journal-Constitution*, March 24, 1998

See also *attention-deficit disorder*.

RMG
Really Mean Girl. See *relational aggression*.

road rage
Aggressive or violent behavior of motorists. The National Highway Traffic Safety Administration estimates that a third of all fatal accidents are attributable to road rage, the most common of the new rages.
See also *rage*.

road rage by proxy
Vicarious *road rage* resulting from merely witnessing a traffic incident, as when one driver becomes incensed from seeing another cut off by a third. In 1997 a Durham, North Carolina, driver-education teacher was forced to resign after ordering a student to chase down a motorist who had cut them off, upon which the instructor jumped from the car and punched the other driver.

roid rage
Collective term for the psychological side effects associated with the use of anabolic steroids, including mania, irritability, and mood swings.

romantic love
The idea that young men and women naturally "fall in love," get married, and live happily ever after is a relatively recent, culturally conditioned notion. It began in the royal courts of Europe in the twelfth century, got a boost from the nineteenth-century novel and, indirectly, from the Freudian tenet that sexuality lies at the root of all human relationships. In societies where romantic love is the only socially acceptable basis for matrimony, arranged marriages are judged indecent, but in Japan, for example, where arranged marriages are popular, there is no difference in divorce rates between couples who "married for love" and those whose parents negotiated their union.

Romantic love, at least in its early stages, is a chemical high associated with elevated levels of the neurotransmitter serotonin (which has also been linked to *obsessive-compulsive disorder*). Ironically, though most Americans say they "marry for love," romantic love and marriage are mutually exclusive: Marriage requires commitment and compromise, not dreamy bliss, and the illusion of romantic love ends in disillusion and disappointment unless the participants make drastic mutual adjustments. Hence the 50 percent divorce rate in the United States.

> Romantic love is mental illness. But it's a pleasurable one. It's a drug. It distorts reality, and that's the point of it
>
> —Fran Lebowitz

> Is romantic love illusion? Delusion? An ideal dream? Just as the majority of humankind will continue to believe in gods of various denominations when no actual gods have been sighted, so men and women will continue to fall under the spell of romantic love and to shape, or misshape, their lives to that end. Biologists may grimly describe for us the mammalian underpinnings of courtship, mating, bonding, fidelity (where there is in fact fidelity)—but, being human, knowing full well as the song warns us that "falling in love with love is falling for make-believe," we are the species that demands to be lied to, in the nicest ways.
>
> —Joyce Carol Oates, *The New York Times Magazine,*
> April 19, 1999

> They were lingering over the good-bye like two people who've met in a museum and are negotiating the next half hour, that crucial time to have a drink and either say good-bye or mess up each other's lives for six months.
>
> —Michael Tolkin, *The Player* (1988)

> When you're in love it's the most glorious two-and-a-half days of your life.
>
> —Richard Lewis

The concept of romantic love is what gets in the way of happiness. It truly always poisons the well, because it makes the received world seem lackluster or inadequate by comparison.

—Harlan Ellison

Juliet's so happy and in love, but at the same time so sad and lonely. She's totally neurotic. I could really relate.

—Alicia Silverstone, on Shakespeare's *Romeo and Juliet*

Tristan and Isolde were lucky to die when they did. They'd have been sick of all that rubbish in a year.

—Robertson Davies

Rorschach inkblot test

Widely used clinical tool in which the subject interprets ambiguous inkblot pictures and experts analyze the responses to create a personality portrait. Though the Rorschach is still valued by many psychologists and used by countless clinics, schools, courts, and businesses to make crucial decisions about people's lives, the test has been exposed as pseudoscience having more in common with astrology or palm reading than rigorous clinical psychology. It has proven worthless for detecting personality traits, tends to misdiagnose normal people as disturbed, and often fails to detect serious mental *disorders*.

Man to psychiatrist after Rorschach test: "*I'm* sick? *You're* the one with the dirty pictures!"

—Anonymous

S

sacred sighting

Alleged spontaneous appearance of religious figures or themes in unusual places, such as an image of the Virgin Mary on the window of an office building in Clearwater, Florida, or on a subway wall in Mexico City. Manifestations can also take the form of food, as with the "nun bun," a pastry in the exact likeness of Mother Teresa, or a slice of tomato that a fourteen-year-old British girl claimed spelled out (in Arabic): "There is only one God and Muhammad is the [sic] messenger." ("God made me buy that tomato," the girl told reporters.) In rare cases a celebrity is depicted rather than a deity, as with a photograph of Shirley MacLaine that allegedly "weeps for future disasters to befall California and the entire region of the universe."

sadism with scruples

Term coined by critic Richard Corliss to describe the righteous violence perpetrated by heroes against villains on TV and in movies.

sadomasochism

Mutual sexual pleasure between a sadist and a masochist.

> A sadist was sued for divorce by his masochist wife for spousal nonabuse, but the husband claimed he was just giving her what she didn't want.
>
> —Howard Ogden, *Pensamentoes, Volume II* (2003)

safety device

Term coined by German-born American psychiatrist Karen
Horney (1885–1952) to describe the neurotic contrivances peo-
ple use to protect themselves from life's vicissitudes.
See also *defense mechanism.*

Salinger, J(erome) D(avid) (1919–)

Hermetic writer and cult figure whose works include short stories and the bestselling novel, *The Catcher in the Rye* (1951), a
chronicle of *adolescent angst* and rebellion.

sanity/insanity

Arbitrary distinction based on shifting standards.

> Who then is sane?
>
> —Horace, *Satires II*

> I doubt if a single individual could be found from the whole of
> mankind free from some form of insanity. The only difference is
> one of degree. A man who sees a gourd and takes it for his wife
> is called insane because this happens to very few people.
>
> —Erasmus

> A man who is "of sound mind" keeps the inner madman under
> lock and key.
>
> —Paul Valéry

> In individuals, insanity is rare; but in groups, parties, nations,
> and epochs it is the rule.
>
> —Friedrich Nietzsche, *Beyond Good and Evil* (1909)

> Insanity: a perfectly rational adjustment to an insane world.
>
> —R. D. Laing

Only the insane take themselves quite seriously.

—Max Beerbohm

Where does the violet tint end and the orange tint begin? Distinctly we see the difference of the colors, but where exactly does the one first blending enter into the other? So with sanity and insanity.

—Herman Melville

Insane people are always sure they're just fine. It's only the sane people who are willing to admit they're crazy.

—Nora Ephron, *Heartburn* (1983)

When we remember that we are all mad, the mysteries disappear and life stands explained.

—Mark Twain

sarcasm
Cutting, ironic wit.

We are suffering from too much sarcasm.

—Marianne Moore

I would have answered your letter sooner, but you didn't send one.

—Goodman Ace

scaffolding
Smothering support and protection of *adultolescents* by their parents.

schadenfreude
Malicious pleasure in the misfortune of others, erroneously thought by moralists to be reprehensible.

It's a German word. There's no direct translation. It means man's need to delight in the discomfort of others. Leave it to the Germans to concoct an intricate glossary of pain terminology.

—Dennis Miller

A pleasant feeling is always generated by the demise of a celebrity. It proves to the envious that, ultimately, the stars are only our equals, or we theirs if we can just find a significant way to die.

—Quentin Crisp

Isn't it a good feeling when you read the tabloids and realize that a lot of famous people are just as fucked up as you are?

—George Carlin

Whenever a friend succeeds, a little something in me dies.

—Gore Vidal

See also *hathos*.

schizophrenia
General term for a group of psychotic *disorders* characterized by hallucinations, delusions, and withdrawal from reality.

If you talk to God, you are praying; if God talks to you, you have schizophrenia. If the dead talk to you, you are a spiritualist; if God talks to you, you are a schizophrenic.

—Thomas Szasz

Roses are red, Violets are blue.
I'm schizophrenic, and so am I.

—Oscar Levant

security

Freedom from danger, doubt, or anxiety.

> Security is mostly a superstition. It does not exist in nature. . . .
> Life is either a daring adventure or nothing.
> —Helen Keller, *The Open Door* (1957)

> Security is when everything is settled, when nothing can hap-
> pen to you; security is the denial of life.
> —Germaine Greer, *The Female Eunuch* (1971)

> The only security is courage.
> —François Duc de La Rochefoucauld, *Maxims* (1665)

> The only security is ignorance.
> —Howard Ogden, *Pensamentoes, Volume II* (2003)

Seinfeld

One of the most successful TV sitcoms of all time (1990–1998),
cocreated by Jerry Seinfeld and *Larry David*. The "show about
nothing" focused on New York neurotics Jerry (Jerry Seinfeld),
George (Jason Alexander), Elaine (Julia Louis-Dreyfus), and
Kramer (Michael Richards), all of whom are glib, shallow, immature, narcissistic, calculating, condescending, cynical, quibbling, cowardly losers. Not that there's anything *wrong* with
that.

See also *Newyorkitis*.

> TIMMY: Did you just double-dip that chip?
> GEORGE: Excuse me?
> TIMMY: You double-dipped the chip.
> GEORGE: Double-dipped? What are you talking about?
> TIMMY: You dipped the chip, you took a bite, and you dipped again.

GEORGE: So?

TIMMY: That's like putting your whole mouth right in the dip.
Look, from now on when you take a chip, just take one dip and
end it.

GEORGE: Well, I'm sorry Timmy, but I don't dip that way.

TIMMY: Oh, you don't, huh?

GEORGE: No. You dip the way you want to dip, I'll dip the way I
want to dip.

—*Seinfeld*, "The Implant"

self, the

In Western cultures, especially the United States, the object of
preoccupation, if not worship, and the raison d'être of *psychoanalysis*.

I count him braver who overcomes his desires than him who
conquers his enemies, for the hardest victory is over self.

—Aristotle

I'm such a cliché to myself that sometimes it's horrible for me
to address my own story.

—Carrie Fisher

We feel safe, huddled within human institutions—churches,
banks, madrigal groups—but these concoctions melt away at the
basic moment. The self's responsibility, then, is to achieve rap-
port if not rapture with the giant, cosmic other: to appreciate,
let's say, the walk back from the mailbox.

—John Updike, *Self-Consciousness* (1987)

This is what I believe: That I am I. That my soul is a dark forest. That my known self will never be more than a little clearing
in the forest. That gods, strange gods, come forth from the forest into the clearing of my known self, and then go back. That I

must have the courage to let them come and go. That I will never let mankind put anything over on me, but that I will try always to recognize and submit to the gods in me and the gods in other men and women. There is my creed.

—D. H. Lawrence

self-affirmation

The practice of declaring something about oneself to be true in an effort to make it true. A hundred years ago the French psychologist Émile Coué advised patients to repeat, over and over, "Every day, in every way, I am getting better and better," and self-affirmation has been a mainstay of *pop psychology* ever since. It may be that reciting affirmations in order to produce desired results, however, is like wagging the tail of a dog in order to make it happy.

See also *self-esteem; Smalley, Stuart.*

self-consciousness

Extreme self-awareness.

Inspiration may be a form of superconsciousness, or perhaps of subconsciousness—I wouldn't know. But I am sure it is the antithesis of self-consciousness.

—Aaron Copland

"Know thyself"—a maxim as pernicious as it is odious. A person observing himself would arrest his own development. Any caterpillar who tried to "know himself" would never become a butterfly.

—André Gide, *Les Nouvelles Nourritures* (1935)

The secret of human happiness is not in self-seeking but in self-forgetting.

—Theodore Reik, *The New York Times,* January 1, 1970

In school we had a name for guys trying to get in touch with themselves.

—P. J. O'Rourke

self-conversation

A popular activity also known as "internal dialogue."

I like to talk to myself because I like to deal with a better class of people.

—Jackie Mason

self-delusion

The act of fooling oneself about important matters, which Freud termed "a universal trait of the species." Indeed, the human capacity for self-delusion is apparently limitless.

Once considered a handicap, a talent for self-delusion may be a useful marital skill: A 1998 University of Florida *study* of several hundred Los Angeles–area married couples found that those most likely to say they were "satisfied" or "happily married" were those who intentionally misremembered the past as worse than it was in order to make the present seem better by comparison. The *study* concluded that contrary to the conventional wisdom, "self-delusion may actually be a more accurate indicator of successful marriage than good communication or truthful, open relationships."

We tell ourselves stories in order to live.

—Joan Didion, *The White Album* (1990)

The final delusion is the belief that one has lost all delusions.

—Maurice Chapelain

self-destructive
psychobabble for "stupid."

self-discipline
Quaint notion involving control of one's conduct, even includ-
ing voluntary sacrifice, in order to "improve" oneself.
See also *self-esteem.*

self-esteem
Sense of self-worth. Once thought a character trait, self-esteem
has become an end in itself and perhaps the most popular concept in modern psychology. It is an article of faith in the social
sciences that high self-esteem is the sine qua non of success and
that low self-esteem is at the root of antisocial behavior.

The enhancement of self-esteem is the Holy Grail of *political
correctness* and a secular sacrament in American public schools,
where high self-esteem is now more important than academic
achievement and where students line up every day and recite: "I
am a good person, I am an important person." Originally in-
tended as a boost for inner-city students, self-esteem has become a crutch to explain away low achievement and a presumed
panacea for a range of social ills, including addiction, depression,
obesity, and dysfunctional relationships.

The philosopher and psychologist William James coined the
term in the 1890s, but it didn't really catch on until 1986, when the
state of California created a "task force" to promote it. John Vas-
concellos, the California legislator behind its formation, compared
the effort to that of NASA and the Atomic Energy Commission.
The idea spread. High self-esteem was touted by media, politicians, and the psychotherapy industry as a virtual birthright, and
self-esteem-enhancing programs proliferated across the nation.

According to its "empowering Web site," the National Association for Self-Esteem was established "to fully integrate self-
esteem into the fabric of American society." There are links to

hundreds of "esteeming Web sites," and to *Self-Esteem Today Magazine,* self-esteem books, tapes, and CD's, and self-esteem "encouragement cards" with such messages as:

Stand tall. You did great!

You try so hard. I'm always impressed.

Be confident. You can do it. CHARGE!

Like the fragrance of a rose, you are unforgettable! I love you!

You are # 1! I believe in you. SOAR!

Relax. Enjoy. You did a great job!

Like a fountain, you bring me so much joy!

You are so colorful! You are so precious to me.

Great things await you. Just take the first step!

Congratulations on your monumental achievement! You are awesome!

Keep up the good work! You are so talented!

In the 1940s, clinical *studies* conducted by Abraham Maslow correlated self-esteem with marital happiness. In the 1960s University of Maryland sociologist Morris Rosenberg linked low self-esteem with anxiety and depression and devised a self-esteem evaluation scale that is still widely used, and includes listings such as "All in all, I am inclined to feel that I am a failure."

There is also a separate "body-esteem scale" with such variables as "appearance of stomach" and "body scent," and a wide variety of other measuring instruments with such names as "The Tennessee Self-Concept Scale," "The Inferred Self-Concept Scale," "Sherwood's Self-Concept Inventory," and "The Twenty Statements."

In the 1970s, the writer Nathaniel Branden pronounced self-esteem a basic human need, "the single most significant key to human behavior" (his formula: "self-confidence + self-respect = self-esteem"), and feminists seized on the idea that female equality could not be achieved without raising female self-esteem (through, among other means, assertiveness training). In *Revolution from Within: A Book of Self-Esteem* (1992), Gloria Steinem placed self-esteem in a broader context, linking it with the plight of such oppressed groups as women, African Americans, and indigenous peoples.

Self-esteem has become a core tenet of clinical and experimental psychology and a guiding principle for therapists of virtually every stripe. It is also a vast industry, with the annual publication of dozens of parenting manuals and "I am special" books, countless references in the mass media, and thousands of articles on the relationship between self-esteem and such disparate factors as "birth experience," bike riding, dolls, video games, scouting, camping, flying, nun abuse (by priests), customer service, LASIK surgery, and Oil of Olay. It has even been suggested that the motivation of the 9/11 terrorists was not religious or political, but personal: They wanted to die because of low self-esteem and terrorism provided the perfect solution.

But here's the rub: *Studies* find no correlation between levels of self-esteem and achievement. None. It turns out that losers, thugs, and scumbags have high self-esteem, too. After years of study, the California task force could demonstrate no link between low self-esteem and drug abuse, teen pregnancy, or poor academic performance. In fact, according to research by Nicholas Emler of the London School of Economics and others, there is no evidence that low self-esteem is harmful in any way. Indeed, people with low self-esteem may do better in life because they try harder. Nor is there any evidence that low self-esteem causes the social damage ascribed to it. Contrary to the popular belief that the better we feel about ourselves the better we do in life, data suggest that overemphasis on self-esteem has produced poorly educated, depressed, violent, drug-abusing children. In various *studies,* people with high self-esteem were more likely to administer corporal punishment to others than their less self-esteemed counterparts. In a University of Michigan *study* comparing the math achievement of Asian and American fifth-graders, the Asian students scored considerably higher than their American counterparts, yet the Americans professed far greater self-esteem.

Praising children merely to make them feel good regardless of their actual performance sets them up for a rude awakening. Telling them they can "do anything" is a cruel deception because, of course, they can't. Some experts even suggest that children actually need to experience at least some disappointment or frustration in order to learn effective coping strategies. In short, self-esteem, like respect, cannot be decreed, commanded, or bestowed, it must be earned through meeting challenges and accomplishing such goals as learning how to read and write.

Most people's self-esteem isn't low enough.
                    —Howard Ogden, *Pensamentoes, Volume II* (2003)

Anyone who even asks the question of whether he has sufficient self-esteem is, ipso facto, a lost soul. Whatever answer is given, the person is in trouble, in a state of profound error and confusion. It is a sign of our increasing self-obsession, of the narrowing of our emotional, spiritual, and intellectual horizons, that a concept such as self-esteem should have assumed such importance and become central to so many kinds of therapy.
                    —Theodore Dalrymple, *New Statesman,* August 16, 1999

The psychotherapy industry . . . would take a huge hit were self-esteem to be reexamined. After all, psychology and psychiatry are predicated upon the notion of the self, and its enhancement is the primary purpose of treatment.

—Lauren Slater, *The New York Times Magazine,*
February 3, 2002

The worst sickness known to man or woman, because it says, "I did well, therefore I am good," which means that when I do badly—back to shithood for me.

—Albert Ellis, *The New Yorker,* October 13, 2003

A really BAD idea is buying six cassettes promising to develop your *Power of Self-Esteem,* and after listening to them and believing them, conceiving that you are really good. Your friends will soon indicate how mistaken you are, and then you'll be back where you started, only poorer by $49.50 + $3.50 shipping charge.

—Paul Fussell, *BAD or, the Dumbing of America* (1991)

Sometimes something can make you feel good and not be good for others.

—Wendy Kaminer, *USA Today,* May 26, 1992

Anyone honestly happy with himself is a fool. (It is not a good idea to be terminally miserable about yourself, either.)

—William Gass, "The Art of Self: Autobiography in an Age of Narcissism," *Harper's,* May 1994

Self-esteem is a myth. If everybody grows up with high self-esteem, who's going to dance in our strip clubs?

—Greg Giraldo

Suggested bumper sticker: We Are the Proud Parents of a
Child Whose Self-Esteem Is Sufficient That He Doesn't Need
Us Advertising His Minor Achievements on the Bumper of
Our Car.

—George Carlin

See also *self-hating Jew.*

self-hating Jew

A Jew who wishes he wasn't a Jew. Perhaps more an accusation
than a phenomenon, almost always leveled by one Jew at another. But there are one or two documented cases: *Sigmund
Freud* was born of Eastern European Jews yet he considered
them riffraff, and the legendary Hollywood mogul Harry Cohn
smoked in synagogue, went to work on Yom Kippur, and revered
the fascist dictator Benito Mussolini. When asked to contribute
to a Jewish relief agency after the Second World War, Cohn
replied, "Relief for the Jews? How about relief *from* the Jews! All
the trouble in the world is caused by Jews and Irishmen."

I hate myself, but it has nothing to do with being Jewish!

—Larry David on *Curb Your Enthusiasm*,
when accused of being
a self-loathing Jew

self-help

Attempted self-improvement through use of books, tapes, programs, *motivation seminars,* etc. Since the 1980s, self-help
books, especially on *pop psychology,* human potential, and recovery, have proliferated with what Fran Lebowitz calls "a rate of
speed traditionally associated with the more unpleasant amoebic
disorders." "Self-help" is typically the largest section in any full-
service book store.

Self-help usually focuses on that negative quadrant of your life, the thing that isn't working. And the more you define yourself by that narrow little piece that's out of whack, the greater the chances that you're going to stay out of whack.

— Carol Kinsey Goman, clinical psychologist

I've been pretty offended by the self-help books. I find people buy them like they use drugs. They figure if they listen to the tape or go through some kind of list, they're automatically going to be healed—and the effort that goes into having character, courage and conscience doesn't need to be taken. . . . I find most of the self-help books lay out phony, constructed-out-of-imagination syndromes like codependency, and put it in terms where you don't have to feel the slightest bit bad about any of your choices or attitudes, something that came upon you or something somebody else did to you. You're sort of a hero no matter what you've done.

—Laura Schlessinger,
Los Angeles Daily News, March 16, 1995

These people who read self-help books. Why do so many people need help? Life is not that complicated. You go to work, you eat three meals, you take one good shit, and you go back to bed. What's the fuckin' mystery? The part I really don't understand, if you're lookin' for self-help, why would you read a book written by somebody else? That's not "self-help," that's "help." There's no such thing as "self-help." If you did it yourself, you didn't *need* help! You did it *yourself!*

—George Carlin

See also *motivation seminar, psychobabble, recovery movement.*

self-love

Once forbidden—or at least discouraged—it is now the Greatest Love of All.

> To love oneself is the beginning of a lifelong romance.
>
> —Oscar Wilde

self-medication

The act of taking prescription drugs not prescribed by a doctor, or using other mood-altering substances to assuage unwanted feelings. Famous self-medicators: Elvis Presley, Rush Limbaugh, Marcel Proust, Judy Garland, and Lenny Bruce, who said of his drug addiction, "I'll die young, but it's like kissing God."

> I always wanted to blunt and blur what was painful. My idea [in taking drugs] was pain reduction and mind expansion, but I ended up with mind reduction and pain expansion.
>
> —Carrie Fisher

self-mutilation

See *body piercing*.

self-pity

Inordinate or indulgent pity for oneself.

> Never feel self-pity, the most destructive emotion there is. How awful to be caught up in the terrible squirrel cage of self.
>
> —Millicent Fenwick

> Self-pity—it's the only pity that counts.
>
> —Oscar Levant

self-realization
Fulfillment of one's potential, now not only a goal, but also a birthright.

self-rejection
Disdain for oneself.

A man cannot be comfortable without his own approval.
—Mark Twain

My inner self was a house divided against itself.
—St. Augustine

I'm not into character assassination, except my own.
—Carrie Fisher

I am married to Beatrice Salkeida, painter. We have no children except me.
—Brendan Behan

My boyfriend calls me "princess," but I think of myself more along the lines of "monkey" and "retard."
—Alicia Silverstone

I've always loathed rich people, so I've become a person who I've loathed. And I loathed myself even when I wasn't that person, which makes it doubly difficult, if you can follow all that.
—Larry David, "The Power of Self-Loathing" by David Noonan, *The New York Times Magazine*, April 12, 1998

Self-love, my liege, is not so vile a sin
As self-neglecting.
—William Shakespeare, *Henry V*

self-respect
Approval of one's own conduct or character. Once a useful standard, self-respect has been eclipsed by the concept of *self-esteem.*

self-sabotage (formerly "asking for trouble")
Psychobabble for treacherous action against one's own interests. Psychologists have developed a profile of self-saboteurs: Raised in unhappy homes and pushed toward conspicuous accomplishment by insecure parents, as adults they have repressed rage, immature egos, and unhealthy appetites for risk. The more they achieve, the more they feel unworthy of their success, until the anxiety is so unbearable that they unconsciously contrive to rid themselves of the burden.

President Clinton's liaison with a White House intern young enough to be his daughter is often cited as a classic example of *self-sabotage:* Did he really think he could get away with sending gifts, leaving sappy messages on her answering machine, and indulging in phone sex at a time when a sanctimonious prosecutor was after him? Of course not. Deep down, according to the self-sabotage theory, Clinton wanted to undermine his own presidency.

serenity
Highly sought-after but seldom-attained state of tranquility or peace of mind.

> I do not want the peace that passeth understanding. I want the understanding which bringeth peace.
>
> —Helen Keller

> When we are unable to find tranquility within ourselves, it is useless to seek it elsewhere.
>
> —François Duc de La Rochefoucauld, *Maxims* (1665)

There is a calm that comes from the absence of electricity. I think the body recognizes and reacts to being encased in a structure through which electricity is flowing. I think the body, in some way, pulsates sympathetically with the electricity, and that the absence of electricity permits the reemergence of a natural calm.

—David Mamet, "The Cabin"

People wish to be settled: only so far as they are unsettled is there any hope for them.

—Ralph Waldo Emerson, *Essays, First Series* (1841)

serial marriage syndrome
Serial monogamy made legal. The serial marriage Hall of Fame includes King Henry VIII (6), Mickey Rooney (9), and Elizabeth Taylor Hilton Wilding Todd Fisher Burton Burton Warner Fortensky (8).

I'm the only man in the world whose marriage license reads, "To Whom It May Concern."

—Mickey Rooney

I never married anybody I didn't think I loved.

—Bette Davis

Always a bride, never a bridesmaid.

—Oscar Levant of Elizabeth Taylor

Second marriage is the triumph of hope over experience.

—H. L. Mencken

serial monogamy
Relationship Russian roulette.
See also *serial marriage syndrome.*

sex addiction

Uncontrollable urge to engage in repeated sexual acts.

> Ann Landers said that you're addicted to sex if you have sex
> more than three times a day, and that you should seek profes-
> sional help. I have news for Ann Landers: The only way I am
> going to get sex three times a day is if I seek professional help.
>
> —Jay Leno

sex and violence

Twin pillars of American cinema.

> Always put sex and violence in your films. That way, even if it's
> no good at least somebody will want to see it.
>
> —John Waters

sex change

See *transsexual.*

sexual perjury

According to *Seinfeld,* mendacity in the context of a sexual relationship.

> The woman had an orgasm under false pretenses. That's sexual
> perjury!
>
> —Jerry, in *Seinfeld,* "The Mango"

shame (archaic)

Strong sense of embarrassment, dishonor, or disgrace caused by
awareness of having done wrong. Once a useful social con-
straint, in the age of *psychobabble* shame is deemed "toxic."

> Western culture, led by American popular culture, is rapidly re-
> moving central shaming events that developed over generations

and replacing them with often trivial and short-lived concerns. Instead of viewing shame as a powerful socializing device, we see it as a hindrance to individual fulfillment. Of course shame inhibits behavior—that's the point. It retards action, it increases reticence, it invokes self-censorship. Of course it makes the individual feel bad. But it does so in the name of a higher social good. Shame is the basis of individual responsibility and the beginnings of social conscience. It is where decency comes from.

—James B. Twitchell, *For Shame: The Loss of Common Decency in American Culture* (1997)

Talk shows have helped transform victimhood into a kind of status symbol. People have been parading their addictions and histories of abuse on these shows for several years. Worse yet, they've been parading the abuse they've inflicted on others. The talk shows don't simply promote victimhood; they promote shamelessness. On national TV, people regularly testify to cruelties, infidelities, and perversities—with apparent pride and pleasure in appearing on TV. "To feel ashamed is bad," a woman on Oprah asserts. (Shame is, after all, a threat to self-esteem.) But what if you murder somebody? Shouldn't you feel ashamed, or, at least—I don't know—maybe a little embarrassed?

—Wendy Kaminer, *Chicago Tribune,* April 2, 1995

You can't shame or humiliate modern celebrities. What used to be called shame and humiliation is now called publicity.

—P. J. O'Rourke

sibling rivalry
Natural competitiveness among brothers and sisters.

As I have discovered by examining my past, I started out as a child. Coincidentally, so did my brother. My mother did not put all her eggs in one basket, so to speak: She gave me a younger brother named Russell, who taught me what was meant by "survival of the fittest."

—Bill Cosby, *Childhood* (1991)

situational intimacy

Intimacy generated by a shared situation rather than a romantic or familial relationship, as when random train or airliner seatmates share their innermost secrets.

situationism

See *Milgram, Stanley*.

Smalley, Stuart

NBC's *Saturday Night Live* character created by Al Franken as a parody of recovery programs. The lisping host of *Daily Affirmations* is a member of AA (Alcoholics Anonymous), COA (Children of Alcoholics), DA (Debtors Anonymous), and OA (Overeaters Anonymous). He begins each show with, "I'm going to do a great show today because I'm good enough, I'm smart enough, and doggone it, people *like* me!"

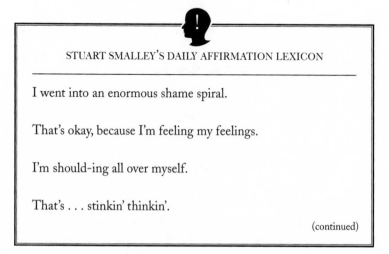

STUART SMALLEY'S DAILY AFFIRMATION LEXICON

I went into an enormous shame spiral.

That's okay, because I'm feeling my feelings.

I'm should-ing all over myself.

That's . . . stinkin' thinkin'.

(continued)

You need a checkup from the neck up.

Trace it, face it, and erase it.

Compare and despair.

Get off the pity pot.

The only person I can fix is me, because it's easier to put on slippers than to carpet the entire world.

smoking

Voluntary introduction of hot, toxic gasses into the lungs as a byproduct of the burning of tobacco or other mood-altering substance.

For decades, in this country and around the world, millions of people used smoking as a way of boosting their dopamine and sharpening focus and concentration. Over the past twenty years, we have gradually taken away that privilege, by making it impossible for people to smoke at work and by marshalling an array of medical evidence to convince people that they should not start at all. From a public-health standpoint, this has been of critical importance: Countless lives have been saved. But the fact remains that millions of people have lost a powerful pharmacological agent—nicotine—that they had been using to cope with the world around them. In fact, they have lost it precisely at a moment when the rising complexity of modern life would seem to make dopamine enhancement more important than ever.

—Malcolm Gladwell, *The New Yorker,* February 15, 1999

This superstitious nonsense of blaming tobacco companies for kids who smoke. Listen! Kids don't smoke because a camel in sunglasses tells them to. They smoke for the same reason adults do, because it's an enjoyable activity that relieves anxiety and depression.

—George Carlin

social anxiety disorder
See *social phobia.*

social phobia (formerly "painfully shy")
Intense, persistent fear of embarrassment, of being judged inadequate in social situations, or of publicly exhibiting anxiety symptoms such as blushing, sweating, or trembling. Involvement in situations such as public speaking, talking to strangers, dating, or using public restrooms may bring on a *panic attack.*

You can't do anything in life. Other than golf, it's very restrictive. The social barriers in life are so intense and horrific that every encounter is just fraught with so many problems and dread. Every social situation is a potential nightmare.

—Larry David, *Entertainment Weekly,*
September 20, 2002

I suffered from social anxiety disorder all my life, and it got so bad that I couldn't talk to people, make a phone call, or even leave the house except for games.

—Ricky Williams, Heisman Trophy winner
and former Miami Dolphins running back

solipsism
Belief that the *self* is the only thing that exists.

solitude
State of being alone or isolated.

> Solitude scares me. It makes me think about love, death, and
> war. I need distraction from anxious, black thoughts.
> —Brigitte Bardot

> Solitude is the salt of personhood. It brings out the authentic
> flavor of every experience.
> —May Sarton, "Rewards of a Solitary Life" (1990)

See also *agoraphobia, loner, quirkyalone, recluse.*

Soprano, Tony
Main character in the hit HBO series *The Sopranos,* about a New
Jersey mob boss (played by James Gandolfini) whose psychiatrist
(Lorraine Bracco) puts him on Prozac for the *panic attacks* he
suffers because both his nuclear family and the family business
(euphemistically referred to as "waste management") are increasingly *dysfunctional.*

Tony Soprano is an emotionally fragile, self-involved thug, a
wiseguy with *angst.* Murder and extortion don't bother him (he
tries to do a favor by blowing up a friend's restaurant), but he
passes out when a family of wild ducks vacates his swimming
pool. Tony's poor impulse control leads to binge eating and ex-
tramarital affairs (he recruits one *gumar* in the therapist's waiting room). Tony also has serious *issues* with his manipulative,
narcissistic mother, who tries to have him whacked for putting
her in a nursing home.

Psychologists and psychiatrists around the country say they
love *The Sopranos* because it accurately portrays what goes on in
therapy, and the show may have revitalized psychoanalysis: Since

the series debut in 1999, therapists report a significant increase in patients, especially men, in an era when HMO's increasingly favor drugs over talk therapy.

Tony Soprano isn't the only screen mobster on the couch: In the feature film *Analyze This* (1999) and its sequel, *Analyze That* (2002), Robert De Niro plays a Mafia boss who spouts *psychobabble* and suffers panic attacks. And according to *Sopranos* series creator and executive producer David Chase, even *The Godfather* can be reassessed from a psychiatric perspective:

> I would say Don Corleone was depressed. Didn't it seem like something very deep was eating at him? He didn't seem to laugh a lot. He seemed like a classic case of depression.
>
> —David Chase

> In a strange way Tony [Soprano] feels the mob has lost its moral center, just as America is losing its moral center. We're all looking for a kind of center, since we can't look to politicians anymore and religion seems to be sinking into a back seat. And Tony doesn't see that moral center in his work anymore. That's why he has the panic attacks. His sense of dread makes him crazy.
>
> —James Gandolfini

> The absurdist view of history . . . suggests that it's people's little quirks and kinks that make big things happen. Modern wars and coups are really the products of mood swings and temper tantrums. *The Sopranos* . . . subscribes to this absurd view. Ruffled pride, paranoia, and childish score settling, rather than any grand plan, determine its characters' fates.
>
> —Stephen Holden, "Sympathetic Brutes in a Pop Masterpiece," *The New York Times,* June 6, 1999

spritz, the

Rapid-fire, stream-of-consciousness monologue pioneered by Joe Ancis and perfected by *Lenny Bruce.*

> Joe [Ancis] was the first to mix languages of totally different provenances, totally different levels of usage, in one phrase. Big intellectual words would rub shoulders in his spritz with old-country Yiddishisms, hipster jazz slang, American underworld argot, and baby talk. Joe's tongue was like a candy crane, carefully manipulated but swinging wild at the last moment to dump into your astonished ear some wholly unexpected sourball or jujube of diction.
> —Albert Goldman, *Ladies and Gentlemen, Lenny Bruce!!!* (1974)

split personality

Psychological *disorder* in which a person exhibits two or more distinct, disassociated personalities.

> LEONARD ZELIG: I have an interesting case. I'm treating two sets of Siamese twins with split personalities. I'm getting paid by eight people.
> —*Zelig* (1993; screenplay by Woody Allen)

stage fright

A species of performance anxiety afflicting amateurs and professionals alike, with symptoms of dry mouth, nausea, heart palpitations, and tremors. Notable victims include Laurence Olivier, *Oscar Levant,* Pablo Casals, Carly Simon, *Albert Brooks,* Linda Ronstadt, Judy Garland, and Barbra Streisand, who, after forgetting the lyrics to several songs during a performance, refused to sing in public for twenty years. Some sufferers swear by Inderal, a prescription drug that impedes the flow of adrenaline.

Extreme cases of stage fright can be devastating. Joe Ancis

was a brilliant but obscure "comedian's comedian" and legendary *spritzer* who regaled the likes of *Lenny Bruce* and Buddy Hackett over burgers and seltzer at Hanson's Luncheonette in New York in the late 1940s, but his stage fright was so overpowering that he never performed in public and remained at best a neighborhood celebrity in his native Brooklyn, while Lenny Bruce used the *spritz* to become famous.

> I'm afraid of getting stage fright.
>
> —Dom Irrera

> There have been times when I've prayed for a bus to hit me so I'd have an excuse not to perform.
>
> —Linda Ronstadt

> Fortunately I don't get stage fright—I just get rest-of-life fright.
>
> —Adam Duritz

stage mother
A woman who pushes her child into show business in vicarious furtherance of her own thwarted ambition. Mama Rose in the Broadway musical *Gypsy* is the archetype, but you don't have to be a woman to be a stage mother, viz.: Kit Culkin, the notoriously *difficult* stage father of *Home Alone* star Macaulay Culkin.

> Stage parents are like rabbits on a highway: bright lights blind them.
>
> —Paul Petersen, ex-Mousketeer

street guilt
Guilt induced by aggressive panhandling.

> There was a time when homeless people held out a cup, accepted your quarters, and said, "Thank you, and God bless."

Now they blame you for their condition. I was in San Francisco recently with my family, and one afternoon we found ourselves walking past a phalanx of street people. "Hey, Dad," a man in a wheelchair yelled at my husband. "Tell the boy about Vietnam! Tell him like it was!"

—Linda Matchan, *The Boston Globe*, November 28, 1999

See also *guilt, survivor guilt.*

stress
Psychological or emotional tension produced by external forces.

Reality is the leading cause of stress amongst those in touch with it.

—Jane Wagner, *The Search for Signs of Intelligent Life in the Universe* (1986)

stress addiction
Inability to get off the treadmill of modern life.

People addicted to busyness, people who don't just use their cell phones in public but display in every nuance of cell-phone deportment their sense of throbbing connectedness to Something Important—these people would suffocate like fish on a dock if they were cut off from the Flow of Events they have conspired with their fellows to create. To these plugged-in players, the rest of us look like zombies, coasting on fumes. For them, the feeling of being busy is the feeling of being alive.

—Thomas DeZengotita, *Harper's*, April 2002

studies
Collective term for clinical trials, laboratory experiments, polls, and surveys heralded by mass media as evidence for all manner

of medical and social hypotheses. "The 1964 Surgeon General's Report on Smoking and Health," the first official acknowledgment of the link between smoking and lung cancer, got wide publicity and may have done more than anything to legitimize studies, which many Americans heed in determining what to eat and drink and what medications to take. Unfortunately, studies show that studies are not always credible, because of bias, faulty methodology, or both. The problem, of course, is that studies are financed by special interests with something to gain from a given outcome, as when banks and brokerage houses commission surveys that conclude that middle-aged Americans are financially unprepared for retirement and should therefore save more and buy more mutual funds (see *retirement panic*).

According to a study published in *The Journal of the American Medical Association* in 2003, pervasive links between drug companies and universities taint biomedical research: Studies funded by the pharmaceutical industry are three times as likely to arrive at pro-industry conclusions than research without such sponsorship. Companies also control the design of studies to insure favorable results and even suppress adverse findings. And researchers are often on the company payroll.

Studies are a source of anxiety because "dueling studies" can cause a whipsaw effect. Thus it now appears that hormone replacement therapy, long touted as salutary for postmenopausal women, may increase the risk of cancer. Margarine, once seen as a safe alternative to butter, has recently come under suspicion. While some studies show fish oil to be good for the heart, others indicate that too much fish oil may actually increase the risk of heart disease, and still other studies indicate that if pregnant women eat enough seafood to get the desired amount of fish oil, they may cause brain damage (from high mercury levels) in their unborn infants. Eggs, once pronounced virtually poisonous, are now okay. Oat bran reduces cholesterol—or maybe not. Red wine is good for you—no it isn't—yes it is. (But grape juice is better. Possibly.)

In reality, any given study is by definition narrow and inconclusive, contributing only a small increment of knowledge on a given scientific question. There's also the problem of interpretation: According to some studies, wine drinkers have a lower incidence of heart attacks. But wine drinkers also tend to have better diets and get more exercise than abstainers or beer drinkers, so the purported causal connection between wine consumption and heart health is questionable.

> According to a study just released by scientists at Duke University, life is too hard. Although their findings mainly concern life as experienced by human beings, the study also applies to other animate forms, the scientists claim. Years of tests, experiments, and complex computer simulations now provide solid statistical evidence in support of old folk sayings that described life as "a vale of sorrows," "a woeful trial," "a kick in the teeth," "not worth living," and so on. Like much common wisdom, these sayings turn out to contain more than a little truth.
>
> Authors of the twelve-hundred-page study were hesitant to single out any particular factors responsible for making life tough. A surprise, they say, is that they found so many. Before the study was undertaken, researchers had assumed, by positive logic, that life could not be that bad. As the data accumulated, however, they provided incontrovertible proof that life is actually worse than most living things can stand. Human endurance equals just a tiny fraction of what it should be, given everything it must put up with. In a personal note in the afterword, researchers stated that, statistically speaking, life is "just too much," and as yet they have no plausible theory how anyone gets through it at all.
>
> —Ian Frazier, "Researchers Say," *The New Yorker*

The Surgeon General announced today that saliva causes stomach cancer. But only when swallowed in small quantities over a period of years.

—George Carlin

See also *junk science, mouse terror.*

Sturm und Drang
German for "storm and stress"; heavy emotion; turmoil; drama.

sublimation
Process of redirecting primitive impulses into more socially acceptable forms, as in the channeling of sexual energy into creative expression. The French writer Honoré de Balzac believed that semen is the very substance of creativity and that its emission constitutes the loss of artistic imagination. He accordingly refrained from ejaculating during sexual encounters, but on one occasion, after accidentally breaking his rule, he exclaimed to a friend, "This morning I lost a novel!"

sudden wealth syndrome
A serious problem for people who get rich quickly, according to San Francisco psychologists Stephen Goldbart and Joan DiFuria, who identified the new neurosis among dot.com millionaires. Sufferers go on spending sprees but always end up empty and depressed no matter how many cars or houses they acquire, and feel guilty over their undeserved riches, all of which can trigger a massive identity crisis or a premature *midlife crisis.*

Sullivan syndrome
Self-doubt suffered by humorists who began to question the value of their work immediately following the 9/11 attacks.

The syndrome gets its name from "John L. Sullivan" (Joel McCrea), the protagonist of Preston Sturges's *Sullivan's Travels,* a 1941 feature film in which a director of hit movie comedies (*So Long Sarong, Hey Hey in the Hayloft, Ants in Your Pants of 1939*) decides that momentous times (the darkest days of World War II) require solemn films, that the world needs meaningful message pictures, not fluff. Despite the pleas of studio executives and members of his own entourage, Sullivan decides that his next film shall not be another comedy, but rather the socially relevant, *O Brother, Where Art Thou?*

In search of material, he sets out disguised as a hobo with only a dime in his pocket. He wants to experience Suffering, and he gets more than he bargained for when he is unjustly convicted of assaulting a railroad bull and sentenced to hard labor on a Southern chain gang, where he is beaten by sadistic guards, chained to his bunk every night, and given solitary confinement in the "sweatbox." His only relief is from an old Mickey Mouse cartoon shown to the inmates in a rural church. Witnessing the audience's uproarious laughter, and surprised at his own mirth, Sullivan has an epiphany: Comedy affords relief from the pain and hardships of life.

Sullivan is eventually released and welcomed back to Hollywood, where, as a result of publicity surrounding his ordeal, the studio bosses are now enthusiastic about *O Brother, Where Art Thou?* But the director does an about-face: His next picture will be a comedy, not a tragedy, because, as he says in the last line of the picture, "There's a lot to be said for making people laugh! Did you know that's all some people have? It isn't much but it's better than nothing in this cockeyed caravan! Boy!"

To the memory of those who made us laugh: the motley mountebanks, the clowns, the buffoons, in all times and in all nations, whose efforts have lightened our burden a little, this picture is affectionately dedicated.

—Dedication, *Sullivan's Travels* (1941),
screenplay by Preston Sturges

See also *humor*.

superego
According to *Freud*, the morally responsible component of the personality that mediates between the *id* and the *ego*.

superstition
Irrational belief that an action or object can influence reality.

support groups
Better living through hugs 'n' confessions. According to a *study* by the European Society of Medical Oncology, contrary to popular belief, cancer support groups do not help cancer patients live longer, and conversation with people who have the same disease does not affect the course of one's own disease. Support groups have been criticized for promoting *self-pity*, and indeed there are now support groups for victims of support groups.

survivor guilt
Irrational guilt in those who've been spared while others have not.

Survivor—the cruelest of all afflictions.
—Chateaubriand, *La Vie de Rancé* (1844)

syndrome
Complex of symptoms that don't quite rise to the level of "disease."

Szasz, Thomas (1920–)

Hungarian-born American psychiatrist whose cogent criticism of his own profession has brought about important reforms and alerted the American public to the dangers of an overpsychiatrized society. He has published over seven hundred articles and two dozen books, including the classic *The Myth of Mental Illness* (1961, 1974), *Law, Liberty, and Psychiatry* (1963), *The Ethics of Psychoanalysis* (1965), *The Manufacture of Madness* (1970), *The Myth of Psychotherapy* (1978), *The Therapeutic State* (1984), and *Our Right to Drugs* (1992).

Szasz is an original thinker who believes that while deviant behaviors exist, there is really no such thing as mental illness, and that thoughts, feelings, and conduct should not be seen as diseases but as "problems of living" that occur because life is inherently difficult. Szasz does not deny that anxiety and depression are real, just that they're diseases in the pathological sense. He contends that mental illness, like spring fever, is a metaphor, and that there is no empirical evidence for the existence of most of psychiatry's myriad *disorders.*

Szasz opposes the use of mental illness as justification for government-sponsored social engineering and assails what he terms the "therapeutic state," the alliance between government and psychiatry to create a climate in which disfavored feelings are "treated" and "cured" as if they were diseases, and bad habits (drug addiction, smoking, gambling, gluttony) and character traits (bigotry, sexual promiscuity, shyness, rambunctiousness) are seen as things that happen to people against their will, a view Szasz contends undermines individual responsibility and invites coercive paternalism. He also opposes forced medication with psychotropic drugs and rejects "dangerousness to oneself" as justification for involuntary commitment to mental institutions. He would also abolish the insanity defense and expert psychiatric court testimony and put those who commit crimes in prisons rather than mental institutions.

SZASZ SZAMPLER

I have tried to make two separate and yet connected points. The first point is that not only is mental illness not "like any other illness," as conventional wisdom now has it, but that mental illness does not exist: the term is a metaphor and belief in it and its implications is a mythology—indeed, it is the central mythology of psychiatry. The second point is that as a profession and as a social enterprise, psychiatry is neither a science nor a healing art but is rather a powerful arm of the modern nation state. The paradigmatic functions of the psychiatrist are inculpating and imprisoning innocent persons, called "civil commitment," and exculpating guilty persons and then often imprisoning them, too (ostensibly for the "treatment" of the illness that "caused" their criminal conduct), called the "insanity defense" and "insanity verdict."

On conceptual, moral and political grounds I oppose these and all other coercive uses of psychiatry. Involuntary psychiatry is an enemy of liberty and responsibility. Morally and legally the only sexual relations we now regard as legitimate are those between consenting adults. Similarly, we should regard only psychiatric relations between consenting adults as morally and legally legitimate.

Contemporary Authors

Definitions of mental illness are prescriptive, not descriptive.

Society, May/June 2000

(continued)

Classifying thoughts, feelings, and behaviors as diseases is a logical and semantic error, like classifying the whale as a fish.

Reason, July 2000

The poor need jobs and money, not psychoanalysis. The uneducated need knowledge and skills, not psychoanalysis.

The Myth of Mental Illness (1961)

By defining the behavior of the individual who exposes himself to the risk of "addiction" as a public health problem, we radically expand the range of legitimate state coercion in the name of health.

Reason, March 1998

In a free society, a person must have the right to injure or kill himself.

Law, Liberty, and Psychiatry (1963)

I have always challenged the "psychoses." Why don't you have a right to say you are Jesus? And why isn't the proper response to that "congratulations"?

Reason, July 2000

The stupid neither forgive nor forget; the naive forgive and forget; the wise forgive but do not forget.

The Untamed Tongue (1990)

T

tattooing
Practice of decorating the skin either by ingraining indelible ink or by raising scars. The earliest known examples are found in Polynesia, but the origin is believed to be universal. The tattoo has served to represent tribal membership, to attract the opposite sex, to appear more intimidating in battle, or to mark rites of passage. Once the exclusive province of urban working classes, tattoos are now de rigueur across all strata of Western society as a personal (and permanent) statement of . . . what?

> It used to be you got a tattoo because you wanted to be one of the few people who had a tattoo. Now you get a tattoo because you don't want to be one of the few people who don't have a tattoo.
> —George Carlin

telephilia
Term coined by critic Frank Rich to describe the pathological longing of Americans, no matter how talentless, to be on television.

> Here's how desperate Americans are to be on TV. They will stand in the rain at dawn hoping to be captured by the camera for a split-second on the *Today* show. They will vie for the honor of humiliating themselves on . . . reality programs . . . including *Who Wants to Marry My Mom?* and *Boy Meets Boy,* in which gay men pick Mr. Right from a pool booby-trapped with nongay contestants. Almost no one can resist the call. How else to account for Brent Scowcroft's appearance on *Da Ali G Show,* in which the eminence grise of national security ended up parsing the difference between anthrax and Tampax?
> —Frank Rich, *The New York Times,* June 8, 2003

television

A prolific source of neurosis.

> Watching television, you'd think we live at bay, in total jeopardy, surrounded on all sides by human-seeking germs, shielded against infection and death only by a chemical technology that enables us to keep killing them off.
>
> —Lewis Thomas, *The Lives of a Cell* (1974)

> As a person who has watched television since infancy, I have always accepted TV as a normal, if dopey, part of life in our culture. I don't really expect it to be interesting or enjoyable. But I'd developed the vague notion that consuming as much news as possible was part of being a good citizen. I thought that by assimilating all that frightening data I was developing coping strategies instead of living in denial. But I was just becoming a nervous wreck.
>
> —Merrill Markoe, *BUZZ*

> It occurred to me that with all the television people watch, most of their acquaintances are actors.
>
> —Arthur Miller

See also *happy violence, information sickness, mean world syndrome*.

Teutul, Paul, Sr. (1949–)

Tattooed, tantrum-throwing, walrus-mustachioed patriarch on the cable reality show *American Chopper* whose primary function is browbeating his son Paul Jr. into meeting deadlines and straightening up the shop. Audiences seem to enjoy the family drama as much as or more than the technical details, which is apparently why a show about the fabrication of custom motorcycles attracts a large number of female viewers.

Creatively, he's next to none, but he's a lazy son of a bitch. And he's real sloppy. He'll just drop shit and leave it there. When the bike's done, I look around and say, "What the hell happened here?"
—Paul Teutul Sr. of Paul Teutul Jr.

My mother and sister have the hardest time out of anyone because it's like your laundry hanging out. My mother doesn't like to see my father yelling at me on national television, and neither does my sister. But [the producers] don't coax us to fight. The fights work, so why wouldn't they use them? It's good television.
—Paul Teutul Jr.

See also *adult temper tantrum, hissy fit.*

therapeutic ethos, the

Elevation of the pursuit of personal well-being and self-gratification above all other concerns, based on the principle of moral relativism (if there are no objective standards, who are *we* to *judge?*). Indulgence replaces self-discipline, and what used to be sins, character flaws, or bad habits are now diseases. Yet, though the therapeutic ethos dominates the social sciences and permeates the national consciousness, depression and anxiety are still rampant.

tranquilizers

Depressants such as Miltown, Valium, or Librium designed to reduce anxiety.

Tamed by *Miltown,* we lie on Mother's bed.
—Robert Lowell, "Man and Wife" (1959)

Tranquilizers are used not only in mental hospitals but in many kinds of institutions where large numbers of people are supervised by underpaid, poorly trained staff members: institutions for the retarded, nursing homes, juvenile detention centers, and prisons. The purpose is clearly institutional management.

—Judi Chamberlin, *On Our Own: Patient-Controlled Alternatives to the Mental Health System* (1978)

transvestite

Clinical term for *cross dresser;* a male lesbian.

I'm an Action Transvestite.

—Eddie Izzard

DIG REVEALS ROMAN TRANSVESTITE

Archaeologists in North Yorkshire have discovered the skeleton of a cross-dressing eunuch dating back to the fourth century A.D. . . .

The skeleton, found dressed in women's clothes and jewelry, is believed to have once been a castrated priest who worshipped the eastern goddess Cybele. Archaeologists say it is the only example ever recovered from a late Roman cemetery in Britain.

The young man . . . wore a jet necklace, a jet bracelet, a shale armlet, and a bronze expanding anklet and had two stones placed in his mouth. . . .

This find demonstrates how cosmopolitan the north of England was.

—BBC News, May 21, 2002

---

trichotillomania

Chronic, compulsive pulling out of one's own hair, resulting in significant hair loss, usually from the scalp, but also from the eyebrows, eyelashes, and in rare cases, the pubic and even perirectal regions. Trichotillomaniacs use fingernails, tweezers, pins, and other sharp objects, which often results in serious skin damage. Hair-pulling is done either as a conscious behavior or an unconscious habit (e.g., while watching television or talking on the phone), or both. Most trichotillomaniacs try to camouflage hair loss with hats, scarves, false eyelashes, even eyebrow tattoos. A given hair-pulling episode can be a conditioned response to a specific trigger, providing relief to built-up tension.

> I used to eat my eyebrows. Until I was eleven or twelve I sucked my thumb and pulled at my eyebrows with my fingers. Sometimes I would put honey or something sweet on them, then pluck them and play with them in my mouth.
>
> —Nastassia Kinski

See also *obsessive-compulsive disorder.*

true believer
One fanatically devoted to some ideology, cause, or individual.

> One might equate growing up with a mistrust of words. A mature person trusts his eyes more than his ears. Irrationality often manifests itself in upholding the word against the evidence of the eyes. Children, savages, and true believers remember far less what they have seen then what they have heard.
>
> —Eric Hoffer

> The most costly of all follies is to believe passionately in the palpably not true. It is the chief occupation of mankind.
>
> —H. L. Mencken

Trump, Donald (John) (1946–) (aka "The Donald")
American businessman and master self-promoter known for his eponymous real estate developments, marriages and divorces, best-

selling business books, brief candidacy for president of the United States (even though he doesn't like to shake hands), and appearances on the TV reality show *The Apprentice* (see *reality television*).

> Do you want someone who gets to be president and that's literally the highest paying job he's ever had?
> —Donald Trump, on his qualifications
> for the U.S. presidency

> Do you mind if I sit back a little? Because your breath is very bad.
> —Donald Trump, to Larry King, *Larry King Live,* 1989

> The man has flair, and New Yorkers will forgive anything if you have flair.
> —Ted Morgan, *The New York Times,* January 1, 1989

Twinkie defense

Pop psychology criminal defense based on "diminished capacity" allegedly caused by consumption of junk food.

In 1977, San Francisco supervisor Dan White shot and killed Mayor George Moscone and Supervisor Harvey Milk in their City Hall offices. At his murder trial, the gist of White's defense was that just before the shootings he had been depressed and subsisted on a diet of Twinkies and Kool-Aid, which deepened his despair and eroded his sense of right and wrong. The jury actually bought it, convicting him of the lesser charge of voluntary manslaughter. White served a six-year prison term, and soon after his parole he committed suicide, possibly after ingesting a Ding Dong.

See also *creep defense.*

tücke des objekts, die

Literally "the malice of things," the sneaking dread that machines are biding their time until they can turn on us and take over the world. Fear of technology has long had cultural expression, from

Mary Shelley's *Frankenstein* (1818) to the homicidal computer HAL in *2001: A Space Odyssey* (1968) to the mechanical irritants that have plagued comedians from Buster Keaton to John Cleese. See also *railway neurosis*.

> The goal of all inanimate objects is to resist man and ultimately to defeat him.
>   —Russell Baker, *The New York Times*, June 18, 1968

U

unconditional love
According to *pop psychology*, the sine qua non of *self-esteem*, i.e., what people crave from their parents, spouses, and children, but only get from their golden retrievers.

unconscious, the
According to *psychoanalytic* theory, the part of the mind containing memories or desires not subject to conscious perception but which influences thoughts and behavior.

> The governing rules of logic carry no weight in the unconscious; it might be called the Realm of the Illogical.
>   —Sigmund Freud, "An Outline of Psychoanalysis" (1938)

> The poets and philosophers before me discovered the unconscious; what I discovered was the scientific method by which the unconscious can be studied.
>   —Sigmund Freud, quoted by Lionel Trilling

> We all agree that Freud did not "discover" the unconscious, and are sophisticated enough to see that it has a history that long

predates him: as the devil that possessed Christians; as the mesmerism and hypnosis that invoked the split, double, and multiple personalities of the eighteenth and nineteenth centuries; and as the theme of "doubling" that informed much Victorian literature and, today, still informs the dumbest plot lines in Hollywood and in psychotherapy. Now connect the dots. In each iteration of the unconscious, some anointed medium—priest, quack, or analyst—claims special access to the darkest, scariest reaches of our minds. For a certain price, he or she can cure you of this demon.

—Todd Dufresne, "Psychoanalysis Is Dead . . .
So How Does That Make You Feel?"
Los Angeles Times, February 18, 2004

My unconscious knows more about the consciousness of the psychologist than his consciousness knows about my unconscious.

—Karl Kraus

undertoad, the
Term coined by John Irving in his 1976 novel, *The World According to Garp*, to express the ever-present specter of personal doom (based on a child's misapprehension about the dangers of swimming in the ocean).
See also *abyss, angst, dark night of the soul, human condition.*

V

vanity license plate
Americans seem compelled to make ostentatious or puerile statements with their license plates, either out of the need to assert their individuality in an increasingly anonymous society, or

out of sheer tackiness. Not surprisingly, Southern California is fertile ground for such self-expression, as evidenced by these actual vanity license plates sighted in Los Angeles:

WEDSRVT
Mercedes-Benz, San Vicente Boulevard

FERN BOB
Lexus, Wilshire Boulevard

2ANEWME
Mercedes-Benz, Pacific Coast Highway

PWRGRL1
BMW, Montana Avenue

HIPHAZN
Infinity, Sunset Boulevard

SOO BUSY
Mercedes-Benz, Pacific Coast Highway

NOZEFXR
Porsche, Sunset Boulevard

STL CRZI
BMW, Olympic Boulevard

JEWISH
Cadillac limousine, Wilshire Boulevard

DBA MOM
Toyota Land Cruiser, Chautauqua Boulevard

KISHMIR
BMW, Sunset Boulevard

H8MYX
Mercedes-Benz, Wilshire Boulevard

MZLNGLK
Lexus, Pico Boulevard

KNEHRA
Jeep Cherokee, Santa Monica Boulevard

L84AD8
Ferrari, San Vicente Boulevard

Some discriminating drivers aren't satisfied with displaying a
sticker that may promiscuously adorn thousands of other
bumpers. They feel the same need to reach out and touch their
fellow motorists, but they march to a different drummer. They
need a message that expresses something unique to themselves.
They need a symbol of their taste and affluence. They need a
vanity license plate. At least that's how I interpret their motives.
My own feeling is that you should get a vanity plate only if (a)
you are a jerk and (b) you want everyone to know it.
                —Stephen Chapman, *Chicago Tribune*, August 4, 1985

victim mentality
In contemporary America, victimhood is a status symbol and
anyone who has ever felt hurt or slighted qualifies as a victim.
People readily label themselves addicted or abused, bare their
souls on talk shows, hear their tearful confessions applauded by
support groups. In short, many Americans no longer feel responsible for their actions.

Upon his conviction for perjury, former aide to President Reagan Michael Deaver pleaded for clemency on the ground that he suffered from alcoholism and depression. In support of Deaver's claim, Reagan biographer Edmund Morris wrote in a letter to the court, "He has passed through the Slough of Despond, and come through curiously purified."

In 2004, two African American women sued Southwest Airlines for physical and emotional distress they allegedly suffered when a flight attendant, trying to get passengers out of the aisles, announced over the intercom, "Eenie, meenie, minie moe; pick a seat, we gotta go." The women claimed they were "humiliated and degraded" by what they said was an intentional allusion to a racist rhyme. A Kansas City jury refused to hold the airline liable.

> I believe the reason I smoke and drink and my wife is overweight
> is because we watched TV every day for the last four years.
> —Timothy Dumouchel, on why he was suing a
> communications company for providing
> free cable despite his request to cancel it,
> *Time* magazine, January 19, 2004

> We tend to forget that a claim of victimization is not a claim of
> innocence. Indeed, people find victimhood appealing because
> they believe it absolves them of their own misdeeds; it imbues
> them with a sense of righteousness. But victimization often
> brings out the worst in people, as the biographies of many vio-
> lent offenders would show.
> —Wendy Kaminer, *Chicago Tribune*, April 2, 1995

Catherine Zeta-Jones and husband Michael Douglas sued the British magazine *Hello!* for publishing unauthorized photographs of their wedding that allegedly made her look fat and frumpy. Zeta-Jones said she was devastated by the photos. Defense lawyers noted that the couple might be concerned about

money: They had sold exclusive rights to photograph the cere-
mony to another magazine for $1.6 million.
                    —John Leo, *U.S. News and World Report*, December 8, 2003

We are not victims of the world we see, we are victims of the
way we see the world.
                    —Shirley MacLaine, *Dancing in the Light* (1985)

See also *political correctness.*

vulnerable
Shorthand for "emotionally vulnerable," a condition that was
once a weakness but is now a strength.

W

wellness
Highly sought-after but largely hypothetical state of tip-top
physical, mental, and spiritual health resulting from proper diet,
regular exercise, and good mental hygiene.

In the Middle Ages, people took potions for their ailments. In
the nineteenth century they took snake oil. Citizens of today's
shiny, technological age are too modern for that. They take an-
tioxidants and extract of cactus instead.
                    —Charles Krauthammer, *Time* magazine, 1996

weltschmerz
German for sadness or disgust over the sorry state of the world.

white coat hypertension
Temporary elevation of a patient's blood pressure caused by the
presence of a physician.

"what-if" thinking
Uncontrollable worrying, often as part of *generalized anxiety disorder.*

whining
Complaining in a self-pitying, childish fashion.

> I personally think we developed language because of our deep inner need to complain.
> —Jane Wagner, *The Search for Signs of Intelligent Life in the Universe* (1986; performed by Lily Tomlin)

> Whining is like having your wheels stuck in snow or sand, spinning and spinning and not ever going anywhere.
> —Lawrence Cohen, *The Boston Globe,* July 4, 2002

See also *kvetch.*

wishful thinking
Confusion of desire with reality, one of the great scourges of humankind.

worried well, the
Healthy people who constantly look for medical problems where none exist, e.g., a healthy woman who fears she may have a serious disease such as AIDS, even though she tests negative and has few if any risk factors.

The worried well look for trouble. They barrage their doctors with countless questions, spend hours online researching supposed ailments, and ruminate endlessly on potential complications. They tend to mistrust medical professionals and disbelieve favorable test results. At the first sign of trouble, real or imagined, the worried well assume the worst: they're not forgetful, they have early Alzheimer's; they're not tired, they have chronic fatigue syndrome; they don't have heartburn, they're having a coronary.

This extreme health anxiety may be related to technological advances in medicine: When there were few effective treatments for most conditions, diagnosis didn't really matter. Now, especially with certain cancers, early detection can mean the difference between life and death.

The onslaught of out-of-context medical information in the mainstream media is another factor. The maddening dual message is that even though nothing is safe anymore, we must still take responsibility for our own well-being and become "savvy healthcare consumers."

See also *cyberchondria, hypochondria, heightened illness concern.*

writer's block
Neurotic inability to write.

> There is no abyss like that of a writer who wants to write but can't and sits around all day wanting to write and not able to and every word he types is horrible.
>
> —James Jones

> Writer's block is a temporary paralysis caused by the conviction, on an unconscious level, that what the writer is attempting is in some way fraudulent, or mistaken, or self-destructive.
>
> —Joyce Carol Oates

> I disavow that term [writer's block]. There are times when you don't know what you're doing or when you don't have access to the language or the event. So if you're sensitive, you can't do it. When I wrote *Beloved,* I thought about it for three years. I started writing the manuscript after thinking about it, and getting to know the people and getting over the fear of entering that arena, and it took me three more years to write it. But those

other three years I was still at work, though I hadn't put a word down.

—Toni Morrison

Not writing is probably the most exhausting profession I've ever encountered. It takes it out of you.

—Fran Lebowitz

See also *hypergraphia*.

Y

yo-yo effect
Vicious cycle in which people lose weight on a succession of diets, only to gain it back every time. Some psychologists believe that yo-yo-ers have an obese self-image and develop eating and exercise habits to match. According to another theory, the extra weight insulates against potentially painful experience (e.g., they fear sex, so they make themselves unattractive). Or, they really love to eat.

Z

zero tolerance
Arbitrary, heavy-handed, but largely cosmetic prohibitions adopted by organizations desperate to control behavior. School districts declare zero tolerance for drugs and violence, police departments mandate zero tolerance for violations of seatbelt laws, the armed forces claim zero tolerance for sexual harassment, and the meat and poultry industries profess zero tolerance for pathogens. But bureaucracies tend to go overboard: High schools

ban dodgeball because it encourages "violent behavior." Elementary school students are suspended for drawing pictures of soldiers. A seventh-grader is suspended and ordered to undergo psychological evaluation for saying he was going to "shoot" another student with a wad of paper from a rubber band, and a National Merit Scholar is jailed because authorities find a kitchen knife under her car seat (the knife had been misplaced during a move between apartments).

Zero tolerance is ultimately zero common sense, because judgment and flexibility are required when dealing with the vagaries of human nature.

> I wish I loved the human race;
> I wish I loved its silly face;
> I wish I liked the way it walks;
> I wish I liked the way it talks;
> And when I'm introduced to one
> I wish I thought
> What Jolly Fun!
> —Sir Walter Raleigh, "Wishes of an Elderly Man"

INDEX